REFRAME

THE MARKETPLACE

REFRAME

THE MARKETPLACE

THE TOTAL MARKET APPROACH
TO REACHING THE NEW MAJORITY

A GUIDE FOR BRANDS AND BUSINESSES

JEFFREY L. BOWMAN

WITH JEREMY KATZ

WILEY

ISBN: 978–1–119–10025–6 (cloth); ISBN 978–1–119–10026–3 (ePDF); ISBN 978–1–119–10027–0 (ePub)

Printed in the United States of America

10   9   8   7   6   5   4   3   2   1

Contents

To my wife, Shewonia, and two daughters, Alston-Simone and Alex-Simone—you made this book possible. You gave up Daddy time and sacrificed moments that should have been yours. And you've done so over the long journey that has brought this work to publication. You've given me more than I could ever have imagined. I hope this book makes you proud of your husband and father.

To my mother, Paulette—you sacrificed your aspirations so that I could grasp at dreams we didn't dare imagine. You made me who I am today, and I thank you for everything.

To my father, Tyrone—thank you for our Saturday morning talks. Your words of encouragement over the years have been the fuel I've used to push for excellence. We caught up enough later in life but not too late for you to become my friend and confidant.

To my grandmothers, Ruth and Hattie Mae; my grandfather, August; and my aunts, Margaret, Renee, and Darlene; my uncles, Paul and Wayne; and my cousins (Bowmans and Striplings).

To Amherst Drive, A Child's Castle, Park Hills Elementary, Spartanburg High School, South Carolina State University, Clark Atlanta University, and everyone who taught me at PepsiCo, MillerCoors, Whirlpool, Dell, Sears, and Ogilvy & Mather ("My Tribe").

And finally, to all of my teachers from the village who gave me the tools to thrive in what we now call the New Marketplace.

Acknowledgments

My journey started in the spring of 1990 when Bobby Hemby, a career counselor at South Carolina State, asked me whether I would like to be an alternate candidate for Pepsi-Cola interviews. Tom Christerphol interviewed me and put me on my way to a great career in marketing, sales, operations, brand management, and corporate strategy. Through them, I gained access to a world I know very well now but not at all then. Through them, I earned a voice in how to build global brands and make a difference in the world. Thank you.

Thank you to Ronald Parker, champion of the diversity effort at Pepsi-Cola. Mr. Parker, your vision for a diverse workplace gave so many of my peers the opportunity of a lifetime. Keep doing what you are doing.

Three books changed my professional life: *Why Should White Guys Have All the Fun?* by Reginald Lewis, *Managing Brand Equity* by David A. Aaker, and *Competitive Strategy* by Michael E. Porter. Each has inspired this book.

None of this would have been possible if it were not for Mr. John Seifert (president and chairman of Ogilvy North America) and Ms. Donna Pedro (chief diversity officer, Ogilvy North America)—two remarkable people who faced the challenge of preparing Ogilvy & Mather for the next 50 years. Who knew a small group of people from Ogilvy's employee resource groups could change the marketing and advertising industry? John, Donna, and the Ogilvy leadership team, you gave us access and a platform to set the agenda for the next generation of marketers and advertisers. We are connected by our ambitions and unwillingness to continue to show up every day and work in an industry that reflects the past.

One of my biggest advocates while at Ogilvy was the original marketing strategy team led by Charles (Charlie) McKittrick. I came to Charlie's notice by way of Andy Jones, Carol Watson, and Asten Morgan Jr. Thank you for paving the way for me. I thank you all for accepting me as I was and teaching me how to be a "Mad Man" who mixed with McKinsey with jeans.

To the original OgilvyCULTURE team—Lou Aversano, Loren Monroe-Trice, Christine Villanueva, Erin Goldson, Enrique Urquiola, Sean Patrick, Sacha Xavier, Willow Gross, Deborah Balme, Ashley Mackel, Robert Henzi, Aaron Finegold, and Rebecca Clayton—thank you for believing in the vision and jumping on board to change the marketing and communications industry.

Talented super producer Sidra Smith has been with me since the beginning of the Total Market conversation. You produced a roundtable when I was not able to make it back to New York because of a client conflict; you produced the very first Total Market Industry Summit, and despite my flaws in planning, you get things done the right way. Thank you for being you and thank you to the participants in the Cross-Cultural and Total Market Summits over the last four years.

To JL—thank you for being the super agent who is the MJ of the literary industry.

To FCB, Cynthia Augustine, Vita Harris, Keisha Vaughn, Carter Murray, and your team for opening up your office and incubating REFRAME: The Brand. No matter how tough the times got, you stayed with us and continued to bring this movement forward.

To Barbara Lippert, Gregory Canzater, Sidney Haynes, Dara Marshall, Malinda Williams, and Veronica Rodriguez—you gave me your ear and pen in the beginning of this journey.

During the winter of 2012 and spring of 2013, there were a series of breakfast and lunch meetings with a group of individuals who would later become the founding partners and members of REFRAME: The Association (formerly known as The Cross-Cultural Marketing and Communications Association): Madonna Deverson, Jeremy Katz, Cynthia Augustine (FCB), Keisha Vaughn (FCB), Vita Harris (FCB), Javier Farfan (Verizon), Singleton Beato (4A's), Lizette Williams (Kimberly-Clark), Dorinda Walker (Prudential), Lewis Goldman (MetLife), Millward Brown (Cheryl Stallworth-Hooper, Ann Green, Susan Hickey, Ola Mobolade, and David Burgos), James Dix (Wedbush Securities), PR Newswire, *Savoy* magazine, Dara Marshall, Laurel Ritchie, Karen Watson, Cindy Kynard, North Star Media, Unvision, Black Entertainment Television, and *Rolling Out.*

I'd like to acknowledge and thank my advisors in helping me form the Total Market Industry foundation for believing in the vision even where there was nothing there: Cynthia Augustine, Vita Harris, Donna Pedro, ET Franklin, Geraldine Moriba, Javier Farfan, Cheryl Stallworth-Hooper, Colin Mitchell, Julie Halpin, Lizette Williams, Margaret Regan, Singleton Beato, Thomas Bartley, Yolanda Conyers, Lou Aversano, Jeff Yang, Michael Farello, Clarence Mitchell, and the vineyard vacation crew.

The very early, early adopters of the philosophy and approach was the "original 67," who showed up at the 2013 Total Market Summit. Who knew your attendance and support would accelerate the idea and practice that there was and is another option to the way our industry learns and practices? Thank you, original 67, for your patience and belief that we could disrupt the industry: Siyad Abdullahi, Salvador Acevedo, Sophia Aladenoye, Danielle Austen, Denise Byrd, Jarek Carethers, Tina Chen, Donal Conn, Linda Crowder, Connie Cunningham, Afia Ohene-Frempong, Alexandra Galindez, Lewis Goldman, LP Green, Vanessa Henry, Stephanie Herold, Heidi Karlsson, Lisa

La Valle-Finan, Bob Linden, Sue De Lopez, Monique Madara, Shelley Martinez, Jose Mejia, Pepper Miller, Shelly Morrizon, Justina Omokhua, Victor Parada, Allen Payano, Alice Pollard and Red Bean Republic, Caroline Riby, Danielle Robinson, Keith Sherman, Lisa Sorensen, Patricia Taylor, Pauline Warren, Anastasia Williams, Katherine Wilson, Cristian Yancey, and Ashley Zapata.

Our mission at REFRAME: The Brand is "To be the global resource for preparing brands and businesses for the new marketplace through Total Market Enterprise training, education, certification, and advisory services for executives and their teams." As you read this book, I hope you take away solutions for addressing critical gaps within your business.

If you have a burning question about how we can help your brand or business prepare for the New Majority in the United States and globally, please do not hesitate to contact us at www .reframethebrand.com or www.jeffreylbowman.com.

Chapter 1

Separate but Equal

The World's Worst Marketing Challenge

Here's a business and marketing challenge for you: You have a product that's intangible and expensive. It requires monthly payments. If things go well, the money your customer spends on it will be wasted. Both the purchase process and every single payment moment require that your customer confront some of the most uncomfortable truths a person can face. There is no possibility that your customer will ever see any personal, direct benefit from your product.

Sounds a lot harder than selling soda, right?

If you haven't already guessed, the product is term life insurance—the stuff that has no cash value and evaporates once the term is over. Its benefits, however, are significant. It can provide a safety net to your beneficiaries in the event of your death—a safety net that is much larger than you'd be able to afford via a whole life policy (the kind with a defined cash value).

But tens of millions of people in the United States have term life—so it can't be that hard to sell. Although this is true, those existing customers have a culturally mediated understanding of term life insurance and the disposable income needed to make it accessible. For them, it's a plus, not a trade-off.

Naturally, the life insurance industry has long targeted this segment. They're affluent and, for the most part, white. They're a great market, except for one major problem: Because they're already well served, the market isn't growing much now or in the future. This poses a problem for the growth-oriented, publically traded life insurance industry.

There is a woefully underserved market out there, one that has a real need for life insurance and is on a demographic growth spurt. But, naturally, there's a problem there, too. This market has little resemblance to the old stalwarts the industry has long relied on. It is less affluent, more ethnically diverse, and often unfamiliar with—even intimidated by—the concept of life insurance. Reaching this audience means staring that marketing challenge right in the face.

The costs of ignoring this audience are high and growing every day. The challenges in reaching them are vast—and expensive to solve. What's an insurer to do?

The answer is simple. To continue to thrive, life insurance companies must reframe their view of the market for their products, going from a narrow focus on the general market to a broad approach to the Total Market. One company, MetLife, did exactly that, and enjoyed extraordinary results. During the course of a one-year campaign, MetLife saw a *60 percent increase* in premiums, fully 40 percent more than its already ambitious goal.

Impressive? Yes.

Easy? No.

Essential? Absolutely.

From the middle of the last century until now, advertising and marketing has divided itself into two big groupings: the general market and the multicultural market. Or, to be blunt, we split ourselves into white and nonwhite agencies. Sound familiar?

The white, general-market agencies (GMA) spoke to the mass market—which was and still is predominantly white. The nonwhite, multicultural agencies focused on individual ethnic groups. Hispanic agencies spoke to the Hispanic population, black agencies spoke to the black population, Asian agencies spoke to the Asian population . . . you get the picture. Given that advertising and marketing is a business of emotional and rational understanding and persuasion, this approach made sense. If you imbue your advertising with a deep cultural understanding, you're likely to connect better to your audience.

For decades, the system worked to a certain extent. The multicultural agencies really did do a better job of selling to their target consumers than GMAs would have done. The whole system might have continued to thrive were it not for human nature. As you've probably noticed by now, this industry division was just another instance of the infamous separate but equal philosophy—only applied to commercial enterprise instead of education. Predictably, GMAs worked with huge marketing budgets, while multicultural agencies divided up a small ethnic advertising pool. When they needed extra funds, they came out of another multicultural segment, not the over-powering general market. Distasteful though it may be, even that system made a certain degree of commercial (if not moral) sense when the white population really was equivalent to the mass market.

That's not going to be true for much longer. In fact, the era of the majority white population has already faded into history in many parts of the United States. Continuing with a fragmented general market/multicultural approach isn't just shortsighted; it's suicidal. The only way to see, appreciate, and sell to the full panoply of America's diverse new mass market is to do for advertising what we did for education five decades ago.

It's time to integrate. It's time to stop carving up our target markets into ethnic slices and time to start looking at the Total Market. When you do, the math changes—dramatically.

Consider the life insurance industry once more. It's known all along that everyone in the United States is a potential customer. After all, none of us gets out of here alive. But knowing that is one thing; learning how to act on it is something entirely different.

MetLife wanted to try. It knew that over the past seven decades, the U.S. population has doubled to more than 300 million people—and that the number of life insurance policies purchased has dropped by 50 percent in that same time. The industry made up for the volume shortfall by selling ever-larger policies to more affluent customers—a strategy that can work only for so long. Rather than watch the industry grow even more elitist, MetLife wanted to see if it could serve a broader market. To do that, it sought out global advertising agency Ogilvy & Mather, where I led the Cross-Cultural Practice. The MetLife executives already knew the demographic realities. Metlife's core consumers were part of a slow-growing segment of the U.S. population. However, there were many people outside of that traditional segment who would benefit from life insurance. They just didn't have a history of purchasing life insurance or any companies marketing to them.

It seems obvious in this case; sell your product to anyone. Everyone dies, so why discriminate with life insurance? But the reality is more complex than that. Educating a new customer base about your product is a major task. It's expensive and time-consuming, but it is a walk in the park compared with educating that new customer base about your *whole product category*. And that's what MetLife had to do. When it looked at the size of the Asian, Hispanic, or black markets in isolation and through the lens of its current product offerings, that kind of investment didn't seem to pay off.

But we helped MetLife reframe how it looked at its market by showing it just how large its market could be. First we urged it to stop looking at the minority segments in isolation. They seem small when viewed on their own, but they become quite a powerhouse when you look at them all together. Now you're looking at a huge and growing demographic.

Second, we added another piece: There is no intrinsic reason why life insurance is affordable only for those who earn more than $100,000 a year. In fact, innovative life insurance policies are affordable even by those with household incomes less than $35,000 a year.

Once MetLife reframed the market that way, the true scope of the opportunity came into focus. There are more than 24 million uninsured or underserved minority households in the United States. That represents a *$15 billion* market opportunity.

Suddenly, a major investment in tapping that market seems worthwhile. But the old ways would not work. MetLife had sized the market as a whole. Now it had to sell to it that way, too.

We knew that selling life insurance had always been what we call a *rational sell.* Imagine your friendly life insurance salesperson saying to you, "And all this protection for your children is only $14 a month. Why, that's less than what you spend on coffee!" There's an emotional component there, too—an appeal to family—but that part was an afterthought. The real meat of the message is the amount of the protection and the price it costs you. Moreover, most life insurance companies depicted white, nuclear families in their advertising.

Rational selling approaches work only when your market is already sold on the need for your product. Appeals to family work only when the family is relatable. Fourteen dollars a month for something vague, uncomfortable, and poorly understood to benefit a family that looks nothing like yours. No wonder life insurance hadn't connected.

If MetLife wanted to sell to today's families, it needed to understand how family looks and acts today. Norman Rockwell's famous illustrations will always be lovely, but they're no longer representative. Today's family is often multigenerational, multiethnic, and gay or straight. It's focused on strongly held traditions and radically new ideas, and it's reflective of culture. Hispanics may find that family obligations transcend generations and borders while blacks are often in female-led, multigenerational groupings of mutual support. Asians have held a firm grip on traditional marriage, the veneration of elders, and broad family interest.

As different as all those family traditions are, one thing unites them: a notion that family isn't some idealized, Norman Rockwell–like concept. It is instead a broad circle of concern. The narrow circle of concern that defined the white, nuclear family has been replaced by an explosion of diversity. As Brian Powell, professor of sociology at Indiana University, has said, "Americans are focusing less on the structure of family per se and instead . . . focusing on the *functions* of family. Families take care of each other. Families help each other. They love each other. As long as Americans have a signal out there that a living arrangement is doing that, then they accept it as a family."[1]

The life insurance category hasn't caught up to this reality, though. The vast majority of life insurance advertising imagery still looks more like *Father Knows Best* than *Modern Family*. MetLife stepped out of that constraint, and like the family of today, it broadened its own circle of concern, speaking to all kind of families—all races, all incomes, and all sexual orientations—at once. It focused most of its attention on the areas of greatest opportunity—the middle market of households earning less than $75,000 a year and the multicultural market—and set ambitious goals. And as stated previously—it blew those goals away.

The Total Market approach and industry has arrived. Unfortunately, most folks haven't gotten the memo.

Like any industry, advertising has its share of conferences and associations. The largest and most influential of all of these is the Association of National Advertisers (ANA), established in 1910.

The ANA is composed of more than 640 companies owning among themselves some 10,000 brands. Together, those companies spend more than $250 billion in advertising and marketing. As you can imagine, when this trade organization makes a pronouncement on something, it carries some weight for our industry.

It has.

In 2014, the ANA joined forces with the Association of Hispanic Advertising Agencies and Asian American Advertising Federation to bring the whole advertising and marketing industry together around a definition of the Total Market approach. They came up with the following rallying cry:

> *A marketing approach followed by corporations with their trusted internal and external partners which proactively integrates diverse segment considerations. This is done from inception, through the entire strategic process and execution, with the goal of enhancing value and growth effectiveness.*
>
> *In marketing communications this could lead to either one fully integrated cross-cultural approach, individual segment approaches, or both in many cases, but always aligned under one overarching strategy.*[2]

Inspiring, right?

Plenty of very smart people contributed to this definition. Not only did three major advertising associations link up, but they also worked with some iconic global brands, such as Clorox, Dunkin' Donuts, and Kellogg's.

Setting aside the grammatical error (did you spot it?), this definition is just a fresh coat of paint on an old idea. This vision of the Total Market approach as the ANA defined it is still invested in the old general market/multicultural divide. It begins and ends with marketing. It cements the sanctity of cultural fragmentation, albeit under a single strategy, and it resembles the feel-good-but-do-nothing diversity programs still metastasizing around the business world.

This definition doesn't end the de facto quota system for advertising. This definition doesn't achieve the Total Market thinking or Total Market success that powered MetLife to such heights.

How did this esteemed group get this so wrong? The answer lies in incumbent structures. The brands that comprise these associations' membership have invested billions of dollars and decades of time into a procurement and go-to-market system that segments and then speaks to consumers in either general-market or multicultural silos. Business has been working that way since the end of World War II.

It's a system I know well.

Separate but Equal

"Do you want to build a business? Or, do you want to feel good?"

I was a little surprised at myself. I hadn't intended to be so challenging in this interview. Still, if Ogilvy & Mather was asking me to come on board to help it and its clients make a major business transformation, I needed to know from the outset that this was a real assignment and not another corporate fig leaf. I was tired of helping clothe naked foolishness.

John, Ogilvy's North American chief executive officer (CEO), glanced at Donna, the chief diversity officer, and paused just long enough to add emphasis to the words he said next: "Jeffrey, we *must* build a business and prepare brands for the New Majority."

I'm a sucker for a good business imperative. I went all-in.

And in the five years that followed, I've been privileged to be at the center of a remarkable new movement in business: the shift to the Total Market approach and industry vertical.

The Total Market approach is a new way of growing brands and businesses for the New Majority. Instead of breaking the nation down into a series of niche markets—black, Hispanic, Asian, lesbian, gay, bisexual, and transgender (LGBT), and so on—Total Market thinking asks us to integrate all of these segments into a meaningful message that appeals to all while appreciating cultural nuances. In other words, it's a new way of engaging with the whole population—not just white people—in mind.

MetLife did that by developing its understanding of the new, diverse family. It found that these broad circles of concern had a family hero at the center—a person who sacrifices for the greater good of the whole. Family heroes caring for others in this way don't expect reward or recognition. They do it out of love for family.

They send money back home, work two jobs, save for college, and wake up in the predawn dark, and they are of every race, gender, sexual orientation, belief, and religion. Met-Life wanted to make life a little easier for all these family heroes to build more secure futures for their families. The advertising MetLife developed drew inspiration from the diversity of families and spoke to them through a shared, emotionally grounded ideal of today's functional (not fixed) family.

This is the Total Market approach in action.

On the face of it, this seems a little foolish. Anyone who has paid attention to business and marketing history over the past few decades knows that companies have been working harder and harder to hone their messages for individual market segments. Every culture is unique and valuable, and businesses have made great strides—and great profits—in recognizing that.

But something has changed. The old approach (called general market and multicultural) made sense when the United States had a demographically and culturally dominant white population. Those days are drawing to a close.

Today all babies born as well as the top 10 U.S. cities are considered *majority minority*. The demographics of today's youth tell us all we need to know. The combined minority percentage of the under-18 U.S. population is projected to become the numeric majority by 2018. In other words, in three years, the youth of the United States will be more than 50 percent minority—hence the term *majority minority*. Although the majority of American babies are still non-Hispanic white (by just a whisker), minorities already account for a majority of births in Arizona, California, the District of Columbia, Florida, Georgia, Hawaii, Maryland, New Mexico, New York, Puerto Rico, and Texas.

Businesses need to adapt to this trend, and they need to do so fast. The old general market and multicultural structure is ill suited to the new reality, and I, for one, am not sorry to see it go.

I didn't get into marketing and advertising to make change. My first exposure to it came when I was just a raw kid knocking around South Carolina State University, one of the historically black colleges and universities (HBCU). I grew up in South Carolina. I attended schools that my parents and grandparents had fought to integrate. I heard the stories of the civil rights struggle and the battle for integrated schooling firsthand from the people who were there. Although the state-funded separate but equal system was anything but that, for the HBCUs, separate often meant *better*.

One of the perks of being at South Carolina State University was its professional recruitment program. Every spring, big companies would send recruiters to our campus to compete for the diverse talent they needed to stay relevant and competitive.

They didn't just look for seniors about to graduate. These companies wanted to get talented kids into the pipeline early— sometimes very early. I was only a sophomore when PepsiCo recruited me into its talent development program.

PepsiCo had an urgent, unmet need. The global beverage giant was converting its franchise-owned bottling companies to corporate ownership. Diversity and inclusion programs were a low priority for these local bottling and distribution franchises. They tended to hire friends and family, all of whom were usually white. Not only was that not going to fly under corporate ownership, but it also was a dumb way of doing business. Coca-Cola had brought its franchise operations under corporate control, and it already had a diverse workforce. That made a difference in the marketplace.

When PepsiCo hired me into its internship program, it paired me with a district sales manager and threw me the keys to one of those big trucks with blue roller shade slides. It wasn't a cushy office job. I was delivering cases of Pepsi off the truck in Knoxville, Tennessee. Plenty of people buy their soda at the grocery store. Some drink it only when they're out to eat or at the movies. But in urban areas, you go to the convenience store to pick up the newspaper, maybe a bottle of Tylenol, a bag of chips, and, yes, a can of soda. The convenience stores and other small businesses were serviced and sold by an individual representative driving a beverage truck. The Pepsi representative would roll up in his blue truck, service the account, take the new order, and bring in the product. It's an efficient system, and a great training ground for young interns.

Now in Knoxville—and throughout the South—the ethnic areas with the largest number of convenience stores had majority black and Hispanic populations. When those coveted delivery jobs were handed from one white bottling company employee to another, cultural representation didn't make much difference. Everybody was equally nonrepresentative. However, when Coca-Cola took over the franchises and ushered in diverse hiring, it gained an immediate advantage over Pepsi. Coke hired talent that reflected the communities they were selling in. Pepsi was slow off the blocks there, but I was part of its catchup plan.

That was my first experience being part of a diversity initiative, and I was delighted that the company's efforts to be more inclusive had a real, measureable effect on sales. I spent several years with Pepsi, and assumed that representative business practices were such good business that every company would soon be lining up behind the idea.

I was wrong.

After college, I got my master of business administration from Clark Atlanta University—another HBCU—and was promptly recruited to work at Procter & Gamble (P&G) as an intern, where I was part of a diversity initiative. This was the golden age of the multicultural and GMAs (which I'll discuss in more detail later)—and while I was at P&G, I saw much attention being paid to different ethnic affinity groups.

Well, *attention* isn't the right word.

At that time, P&G was paying lip service (and little else) to diversity and inclusive commercial programs—and it wasn't the only one. I worked at a number of big brands—Miller, Whirlpool, Dell, and Sears—in various marketing leadership positions, and I saw the same patterns repeated everywhere I went. Companies expressed interest in reaching and selling to every ethnicity. They worked to build a diverse talent pool internally. But when it came time to *spend money*—to invest in distribution or marketing—the commitment evaporated.

During my time in marketing, I worked with both general-market agencies (those appealing to the mass market, which at that time excluded most ethnicities) and multicultural shops (those whose remit extended to black, Hispanic, or Asian consumers). It didn't take a fancy background in demography to figure out where the growth was going to be coming from. Minority populations were already on the rise; the demographic shift we're living through now was evident. And yet when it came time to allot budgets, the balance went the other way. The marketing spend I would direct to GMAs was often 10 times greater than the money directed to their multicultural counterparts. When the chief marketing officer and his team connected with the agency leadership, we'd all head out to a group dinner with the GMA whereas the multicultural agency rated only a hurried breakfast.

The marketing team at one of the companies I worked for had to grapple with a budget shortfall. This brand counted black consumers among its most loyal. But the hard truth was that we needed to increase our marketing expenditure in Texas, California, and Florida. The Hispanic population there was booming, and we were losing out to a competitor. If we solidified our position there, it would have major impacts on our profitability and national standing. Rather than short the already outsized general-market budgets, my bosses elected to divert nearly every dollar of spending from the black market to the Hispanic market. We could, it seemed, market either to our loyal black consumers or to attract new Hispanic ones—but not to both.

I'd have been the first to applaud the decision if it had made business sense, but it was financially counterproductive. Our diversity initiative made the company feel good, but it had no bearing on our behavior in the market.

I saw other companies repeat that same faulty decision. The budget for reaching ethnic minorities was—there's no getting around the term—a quota. All the initiatives in the world couldn't make that number grow, even if it made good business sense.

Diversity and business outcomes seemed happily married when I worked at Pepsi, but by the time I made it higher in the marketing organization of other brands, it became clearer that I had seen a rare exception to the rule.

As the years wore on, nothing appeared to change inside of big companies. They still maintained diversity initiatives and sought out diverse talent but maintained a separate but equal marketing policy—one that was just as separate and every bit as equal as the one in the Jim Crow South my folks had fought against.

But something was changing outside of these big businesses: the external society. The demographic trends were going from noticeable to unavoidable. Hispanic, black, Asian, and LGBT markets were growing—fast. In fact, they were projected to be the major sources of economic growth for the whole nation for decades to come.

When I left Dell, still frustrated by the persistent undervaluing of the marketplace I knew best, I decided that I had to find a way to turn internal company policy into market-facing action.

I was driven to change the market for personal reasons, of course. But I was just as motivated by the untapped potential I saw. It's easy to stick to the old way. It is, after all, what seems to make logical sense: Target your advertising to your customer with the utmost precision. But we're not the same nation we once were. As MetLife found out, society is gradually effacing the sharp-edged boundaries we've lived with for generations. As minority populations become the majority, our culture is becoming one of inclusion. This is playing out right now in the gay rights movement. The push for marriage equality started just 10 years before this writing. Now, it's become an almost-unstoppable social force. Marriage equality is the fastest-moving social justice movement in our nation's history. It epitomizes our national march from exclusion, to tolerance, to inclusion.

As with prior developments, a general market/multicultural structure is unsuited to this new reality. Nor is it suited to the demographic changes that have, in part, brought it apart.

In 1980, the census found the U.S. population looked one way (see Figure 1.1).

By 2010, it had changed (see Figure 1.2).

In 30 years, the white population dropped by more than 15 percent while the black population grew by just less than

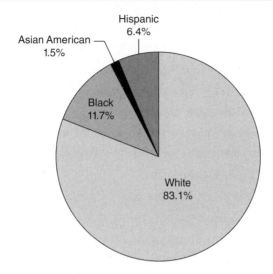

FIGURE **1.1**   1980 U.S. population demographics

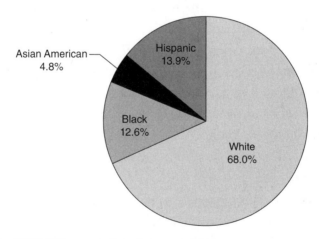

FIGURE **1.2**   2010 U.S. population demographics

1 percent. Asians jumped by 3.3 percent, and Hispanics, the powerhouse minority demographic, increased by 7.4 percent.

The current marketing communications ecosystem isn't flexible enough to reflect this new population structure. In theory, GMAs speak to nearly 70 percent of the marketplace, and multicultural ones cover the remaining 30 percent. But my experience isn't an anomaly. In practice, the overall media spend for the United States is tilted steeply toward the general market: The media buy for that segment chews up 93 percent of a $117 billion industry. So, not only is the system clunky and frustrating for clients, but it's also increasingly ill suited to the task at hand. In a multihued nation, the advertising business looks alarmingly monochrome. As it's presently structured, everybody loses: Clients reach only part of their audience. Advertisers and marketers fall short of their benchmarks.

There are good reasons for this system's longevity. General-market agencies aren't comfortable marketing to minority segments, and multicultural agencies are protective of their turf. But when the minority population—blacks, Hispanics, Asians, and LGBT individuals—makes up more than 40 percent of the market, you can't even claim to *have* a general market anymore. There's a desperate need for a new paradigm. The choice businesses face isn't between general market and multicultural. It's a choice between selling to 60 percent of the population (and shrinking!) or selling to *everyone*.

Fortunately for me, I hit peak frustration just about the same time that Ogilvy & Mather started thinking about how it could start selling to everyone, not just the 60 percent.

Ogilvy & Mather was founded by David Ogilvy, one of the sharpest ad guys the world has ever produced. While he earned fame as a copywriter and creative, he achieved legendary status by writing some of the best-selling advertising books of all time: *Confessions of an Advertising Man* and *Ogilvy on Advertising.*

Both books are still required reading for anyone serious about advertising and marketing. As a result of that founder's DNA, Ogilvy & Mather has a long-standing tradition of not just doing advertising but *thinking* about it as well. That's exactly what John Seifert, then CEO of Ogilvy & Mather's North American division, and Donna Pedro, chief diversity officer (CDO), were doing when they asked me to come in. After we chatted for a bit,

John asked me a pointed and prescient question: "How can we prepare Ogilvy & Mather for the next 50 years?"

You've already read the question I shot back in answer that day: "Do you want to build a business? Or, do you want to feel good?"

If your answer is the same as John's—if you want to transform your brand and build a business—then this book is your road map. This book tells you how you can prepare your business for the next 50 years.

You may feel frustrated by stagnating growth. Maybe you recognize that minority segments have increasing consumer power but don't know how to reach them. Perhaps your own family looks different from the one you see in advertising. If you're a small- or medium-sized business owner, you know your audience is both more fragmented and more unified than ever. Like MetLife, you know that there is a larger potential market out there for you to reach. You know it is the secret to growth. But how to you cater to it without ignoring the rest of your customer base?

How can you grow in concert with America? Broaden your reach while deepening your engagement? Become more targeted even as you outspread your arms to all?

This book will tell you how.

Chapter 2

The Source of Growth

The Underserved Consumer

In 1996, I was enrolled at Clark Atlanta University studying for my master of business administration. This school emerged in its present form only in 1988, following the merger of Clark College and Atlanta University, both of which were more than a century old at the time of the combination. As a business school student, it made perfect sense to me: Why shouldn't the historically black colleges and universities participate in the mergers and acquisitions boom of the 80s?

Clark Atlanta University sits just a short distance southeast of the Georgia Dome in Atlanta's urban heart, in a city that has long had a thriving African American culture. Given that geographical context, you can imagine the enthusiasm that greeted the publication of Michael Porter's May/June 1995 article, titled "The Competitive Advantage of the Inner City," published in the *Harvard Business Review* (*HBR*).[1] Perhaps *enthusiasm* is too strong a word for an *HBR* article, but consider the circumstances: It was the mid-90s. The North American Free Trade Agreement treaty was just two years old, having been approved by Congress in 1993 and signed into law by President Clinton in 1994—and its effects were already being felt. Globalization, one of history's long arcs, was accelerating toward an apex driven by containerized shipping, just-in-time manufacturing, burgeoning communications revolutions, and the Western political realignment that the fall of Communism occasioned. The effect that mattered most to me is known to economists as "labor force migration" and to working people as "shipping our damn jobs overseas."

That result hit the inner city hard. U.S. inner cities had dramatically higher percentages of black and Hispanic populations with household incomes less than $40,000. Good jobs were scarce, drugs were rampant, social programs were shredded . . . and hope was fleeing along with the work. I lived in one of those cities and attended school there. I had worked in one of those cities humping cases of Pepsi. So, when a famous economist parachuted in with a paper showing a private-sector, self-sufficient way forward for inner cities, I greeted it with enthusiasm.

Porter's credentials were impeccable. Back in 1979, he had written "How Competitive Forces Shape Strategy," thus creating the modern notion of business strategy with what's come to be called "Porter's Five Forces." Their impact on academics and business wasn't merely theoretical; his work changed business practice. I thought perhaps he'd have the same impact on the trajectory of America's inner cities.

Porter wrote about the misconceptions behind current national policy on cities. Government largess wouldn't cure the malaise, nor was cheap labor or inexpensive real estate a panacea. In fact, government investment had largely failed; and labor, though cheaper than in the suburbs, was still more expensive than what could be found in Mexico, and Mexican real estate was even cheaper. No, the American inner city's competitive advantage could be found only in what made it unique. As Porter wrote at the time, "My ongoing research of urban areas across the United States identifies four main advantages of the inner city: strategic location, local market demand, integration with regional clusters, and human resources."

Porter's work demonstrated what is known today as a social impact case for helping brands understand the untapped opportunity within the inner city and among underserved and underserviced populations. It's a blindingly obvious argument that nevertheless seems difficult for many businesses to grasp. Lots of people live in dense urban areas. Many of those people cannot afford basic necessities, much less luxuries, because of low incomes. However, they are a large and concentrated potential market. Bring jobs into the urban centers, and a robust consumption market will soon follow. Today, we think about lively urban areas in Chicago, New York, Atlanta, and Memphis. The urban hearts of those cities and others like them are anchored by big sports facilities, trendy shopping and restaurants, and mixed-use streets.

But that wasn't the case two decades ago. The year of Porter's article—1995—was a different world in many respects. The Internet was still a mewling infant. In fact, AOL and Prodigy had just started offering Web access. America wasn't yet trans-fixed by YouTube. Instead, we were enjoying one of our last genuinely communal video experiences—the O. J. Simpson trial. How fitting, given the racial overtones and troubling prejudices that it explored.

The year 1995 was also a time when the electoral impact of minority populations had not yet been felt. Blacks, particularly urban blacks, just didn't vote—or so the story went. And in 1995, that still held a ring of truth. In addition, the landmark 2010 census was still 15 years in the future. It was already obvious that the Hispanic population was exploding. In 1980 (the first year the Census Bureau included the category), the Hispanic population was 14.6 million. It was up to 22.4 million 10 years later. By 2000, it had climbed to 35.3 million, more than doubling its total from just two decades past. Whites still comprised a solid majority of the nation, but a population sea change was starting to become obvious. The white population grew by 7.9 percent between 1980 and 2000, whereas the minority population grew by *88 percent* during that same time—fully *11 times* faster. This growth was fueled in large part by the growth of the Sun Belt states and the great northern migration of Mexican immigrants to the United States.

The technology sector was just beginning its rise in 1995. Emerging companies rushed in to exploit the digital revolution, predictably focusing their products and services on the consumers they knew and understood best: white, middle-class males. Technology also accelerated the offshoring trend. Information doesn't cost anything to ship, after all, so call centers and information technology services headed in search of lower wages.

Business largely ignored the implications of Porter's article. Technology companies widened the investment gap in inner cities

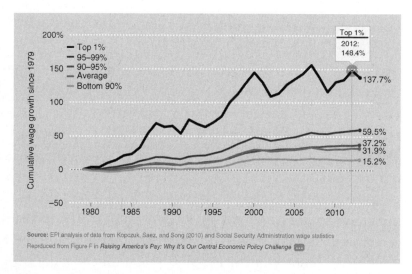

FIGURE 2.1   When It Comes to the Pace of Annual Pay Increases, the Top 1 Percent Leaves Everybody Else in the Dust: Cumulative Change in Real Annual Wages, by Wage Group, 1979–2013

Source: Wojciech Kopczuk, Emmanuel Saez, and Jae Song, "Earnings Inequality and Mobility in the United States: Evidence from Social Security Data Since 1937," *The Quarterly Journal of Economics* 125, no. 1 (February 2010): 91–128, updated through 2013 with data from the Social Security Administration *Wage Statistics* database; analyzed in Figure F in Josh Bivens, Elise Gould, Lawrence Mishel, and Heidi Shierholz, *Raising America's Pay: Why It's Our Central Economic Policy Challenge* (Washington, DC: Economic Policy Institute, June 2014).

and with underserved, underserviced markets. Middle-class jobs fled the United States—and all the while a massive demographic shift was taking place, which rendered those twin business trends completely misguided. These factors led to a massive growth in wage inequality—an issue that is likely to be in the forefront of future political campaigns. How bad is it? Well, look at this sobering chart (Figure 2.1) from the Economic Policy Institute.

To be fair, businesses had made some serious strides since the dawn of the twentieth century. The rich and profound integration of American culture we cherish today would have seemed like a travesty to white America not too long ago. David Ogilvy once said that "Advertising reflects the mores of society, but it doesn't influence them." Judging by that standard, America was an awfully unevolved place over a hundred years ago. The famous Fairy Soap ad from the 1860s (Figure 2.2) pretty much sums it all up.

FIGURE 2.2   This is only one of the many racist ads Fairy Soap produced

FIGURE 2.3 Native Americans were depicted as caricatures or used in punch lines in advertisements for decades—a practice that persists in mascots and logos to this day

Of course, blacks weren't the only ones to be vilified in advertisements. Native peoples were subjected to the same kind of dehumanizing imagery, as shown in Figure 2.3.

Considering how blacks and native peoples were treated in North America, vile advertisements might have been the least of their problems.

In the 1960s, McKinsey & Company published a paper alerting brands to the "Total Market" opportunity, thus coining the term that now, 50 years later, is just coming into wide usage. McKinsey's paper explained that brands and businesses could

FIGURE 2.4 The makers of Jax Beer knew that their audience was primarily Black, and, sensibly, they marketed directly to them

miss a significant opportunity by not addressing the wants and needs of the "upwardly mobile Negro." McKinsey might have coined the term, but a few brands were already paying attention, particularly those reliant on minority customers.

Targeted advertising started to appear, first in print, and then in electronic media. The first TV commercial to target African Americans came from New Orleans–based Jax Beer, a brand that had a largely black consumer base (see Figure 2.4).

The Jax Beer ads were among the first produced for the African American market. Before that, blacks had been shown as figures of ridicule, servants, or just part of the background furniture that made the idealized image of white life possible. One advertiser hardly marked the end of discrimination. And a triflingly few brands were paying heed to the opportunity.

Figure 2.5 The famous and path-breaking Coca-Cola "Bench" ad

You might wonder, What's the point of looking back so far? Aren't we past all that? In many ways, we are. And Coca-Cola was one of the brands that helped get us there with its iconic ad from 1969 (Figure 2.5): white kids and black kids sitting down, chatting, even touching. It's nothing to us now. But in 1969, it was a shocking image.

Advertising integration has come a long way. Today, famous people of every race sell us every imaginable product of the consumer lifestyle. Black figures aren't background furniture; now, they're avatars of manliness, as the runaway success of Old Spice's new brand campaign proves. This series has all but singlehandedly revitalized the Old Spice brand, but as you'll read later, it hasn't worked in the market you may expect. Old Spice created its iconic ad campaign around Isaiah Mustafa, a handsome and aspirational image of the male ideal.

As hilarious and celebratory as Mustafa's unforgettable ads are, they're not exactly free of the legacy of bias—the black man as the sexy, shirtless epitome of virility.

FIGURE **2.6**   *Mandingo* is famous as an example of threatening black male power

Figure 2.6 is a movie poster for *Mandingo*—the defining example of black male virility and threat. Notice any similarities?

So maybe we're not *that* evolved after all. Still, advertising has progressed mightily along two separate fronts. The first is the use of minority figures routinely in general-market ads, even if the results are sometimes cringe inducing, as marketers have had to learn again and again. Intel put out a great high-concept print ad that touted the business-ready application of its Core 2 Duo processors. The ad featured a businessman flanked by sprinters at their marks, which is an effective way to highlight the speed of the processor. Unfortunately, the sprinters were black; the businessman was white. Now even a modestly attentive viewer sees a white dude surrounded by bowing black men. Not cool.

Even brands who have their hearts in the right place sometimes screw up. Dove, the skin care line, which has worked hard to promote an inclusive notion of beauty, blew it in one of their Campaign for Real Beauty print ads. The body was ad featured a prominent before and after image of skin to demonstrate Dove's soothing properties. Unfortunately, the three women pictured in the foreground were positioned in such a way as to leave the reader thinking that the larger black woman on the left was the "before" image while the slender white woman on the right was the "after." Uh, oops?

The other thread of advertising inclusiveness is the rise of multicultural advertising agencies. Global Hue, Alma, Axis, and Burell—to name a few—are major national advertising agencies that control billions of dollars of media spend. But as big and powerful as they are, they retain the habits of a separate but equal world. While it will take some time for agencies to fully make the shift, the run of the multicultural agency seems to be ending.

And in 2008, a national event made it impossible to ignore the rising power of the New Majority any longer. That precipitating event was the 2008 presidential election.

New Majority voters came out to vote in droves, putting to rest the unfounded claim that blacks and other minorities don't vote. And not only did they vote, they also used new technology, new ways of communicating, new ways of building community, and new ways of visualizing data. The technological revolution born in the 90s for the same old white, male consumer was now being repurposed by New Majority consumers to elect—and then reelect—a president of color. Moreover, the demographic shifts that came to light thanks to the 2000 census got a visceral proof point. Barack Obama didn't win the majority of white men—and yet swept to a historic victory.

In other words, America and the world witnessed firsthand what Porter had been advocating for in his 1995 *HBR* case study.

Was the Porter prediction now true? Why was the first data point within the geopolitical landscape? And why did it take us so long to respond to what's obvious when you look at the numbers? The opportunity had been identified back in the 60s! And the play-book for action was already 22 years old.

The truth is that the numbers were not strong enough yet. Business is a remarkably adaptive institution, after all. Nothing can hold it back in the face of an open market opportunity. Business did, however, *believe* it was responding. Multicultural agencies were growing every year, and so were their media budgets. Unfortunately, as I've seen firsthand, multicultural spending has always been underwhelming. For large companies—even ones dependent on minority communities—multicultural marketing investment has always been less than that directed at the general market.

That made a certain amount of sense for a certain amount of time. But if the 2008 presidential election proved anything at all, it was that the New Majority had arrived and was intent on being heard. The general market/multicultural market split was no longer a viable option.

This chapter has looked at these market shifts through the lens of advertising because that's the way most consumers experience business trends. However, as we'll discuss later in the book, the Total Market begins with *business* transformation, not *advertising* transformation. Alas, most businesses still see this in terms of advertising in general and specifically ethnic advertising.

That ignorance is no longer tenable. In 2018—just three years on from the early spring night when I am writing these words—the entire U.S. population under 18 years of age will be majority minority. This is already a $4 trillion market annually. It's growing faster than any other market segment, and businesses that blow this transition will become irrelevant or extinct by the time those majority minority youngsters grow up.

Transforming into a Total Market enterprise isn't just a matter of flipping a switch. Doing it right is at least a four-step process, which we'll cover later. Some businesses will require five. The brands that do make the shift to Total Market Enterprises will be the ones best suited to success in the years to come.

In the next chapter, we'll take a deeper look at the numbers driving the Total Market transformation and show how the general/multicultural divide is no longer viable.

A Timeline of Minority Market Firsts for the Advertising Industry

1827
First ad in black press appeared in *Freedom's Journal*.

1919
First targeted marketing strategy. Claude Albert Barnett's Associated Negro Press provided black newspapers content specifically crafted to their readerships.

1947
First ad by major advertiser. Zenith Radio Company took space in *Ebony* magazine.

1947
First executive hired to help appeal to blacks. PepsiCo employed Edward F. Boyd.

1951
First market researcher for the ethnic market hired. Coca-Cola brought in Moss Kendrix to convert the black audience.

1956
First African American agency founded. Vince Cullers launched Vince Cullers Advertising and set in motion the general/multicultural market split.

1962
First Hispanic agency, Spanish Advertising and Marketing Services, founded.

1968
First African Americans appeared in national advertising.

1974 (approximately)
First consumer research conducted on blacks in advertising.

1981
First Asian American agency, Pan-Com, founded by Young M. Kim.

1984
First Fortune 500 campaign targeted Asian Americans.

1985
Major advertisers started advertising on Hispanic TV.

1985
Minority-owned agency appointed Kodak agency of record.

1990
U.S. census released. Asian Americans became key target for marketers.

1993
First Spanish-language TV ad aired on CBS.

(*continued*)

(*continued*)

1995
First major coordinated general market/Hispanic market campaign launched. Allstate ran general market and Spanish media advertising, using same brand message.

2000
First advertiser had a Total Market strategy.

2002
First major prediction made for moving past multi-cultural marketing to more holistic marketing.

2006
Toyota aired the first bilingual commercial in English and Spanish for its Camry hybrid during the Super Bowl.

2009
Best Buy acknowledged a Muslim holiday for the first time in national advertisement.

2010
Census released.

2011
Walmart endorsed Total Market approach.

2013
The first Total Market marketing and communications industry conference took place.

Chapter 3

What's Wrong with General-Market and Multicultural Marketing?

O n the face of it, nothing is wrong. For the next few generations—perhaps forever—people from different communities will have different cultural associations. I'm a black man from the South. My cultural milieu is different from the one Jeremy, the white, midwestern, Jewish guy writing this book with me, has. We like a lot of the same things and have largely interchangeable slang, probably because our kids are around the same age. We both experienced bigotry, albeit to a vastly different degree. But for all of these similarities, no marketer worth his or her *Ad Age* subscription would ever market to us the same way. Our communities are different. Our tastes are, too. Our cultural references overlap, but when it comes to foods and celebrations—some of the most intimate of our collective experiences with family and friends— we are literally worlds apart. Put simply, we share many traits and behaviors, but we come from fundamentally different places emotionally.

While advertising and marketing tries to cultivate a behavioral response—buying the product, signing up for the service, recommending to a friend, and so on—it does so through the medium of emotion. Humor, pathos, identification, envy, lust—we cycle through the full gamut of limbic responses over the course of one Super Bowl.

If advertising succeeds by eliciting emotional connection, why on earth would marketers ever want to market to Jeremy and me the same way?

They shouldn't. But the general market and multicultural divide isn't only about speaking to different communities in their own context. That system is built on the presumption that these communities are still entirely distinct. But they aren't anymore, and we're awfully late in realizing it. We're like the United States normalizing relations with Cuba nearly three decades after the end of global Communism. The status quo system isn't just dated; it also corrodes value for brands and businesses.

Evolution

David Ogilvy famously said, "Advertising reflects the mores of society, but does not influence them." As America has evolved, the marketing and communications industry lagged behind, reflecting back the light from distant times.[1]

By the mid-1960s, there were remnants of the great migration. Many American blacks had relocated from the South to northern and western states, finding middle-class wealth along the way. As more and more blacks moved into new income brackets in the 1970s, they aspired to assimilate with their white counterparts. They had purchasing power, and brands were eager to get their share. The multicultural agencies spoke to blacks—and other minority populations— because cultural integration was still decades away. And the numbers were small. There were fewer middle-class minorities on a percentage basis, and the populations as a whole were smaller. Small slices of budgets formed and were devoted to multicultural marketing. The general market got the big portion. That made sense for a time, because the minority population just wasn't there.

But it was coming.

Shifting Demographics

Although the general and multicultural divide is still with us, parts of our business model have, in fact, morphed to reflect America's dramatically shifting demographics. Our business offerings now reflect the importance of Hispanics, blacks, Asian Americans, and the lesbian, gay, bisexual and transgender (LGBT) community—also known as the New Majority. Budgets have grown as these segments have ballooned, and the desire among brands for multicultural services has increased. Notice the words I just used—*grown, increased*, and *ballooned*. Although the population has gone up dramatically, the desire and budget for services has grown only modestly. The marketing industry just isn't set up to adapt, because it still uses a model that divides business between general-market and multicultural agencies—an obsolete approach.

And for good reason. In a recent survey, Ogilvy & Mather asked chief marketing officers, executive vice presidents, and directors of marketing a few questions about their level of satisfaction with both the general-market and multicultural agencies with which they have worked.[1] Ogilvy & Mather found they were satisfied with neither—primarily because of the agencies' inability to deliver integrated communications across the two platforms. More than 70 percent of those surveyed rated their general-market agencies (GMAs) a 3 or below on the 1 to 5 scale we gave them.

Ogilvy & Mather then asked the same executives about their multicultural advertising or marketing agency. The results were even worse: 93 percent rated the multicultural shop 3 or below, and 50 percent of the respondents gave it a *1*! This is hardly a surprise, given that most of the people surveyed didn't have a multicultural agency of record—a go-to shop—and instead used one on a project-by-project basis. Executives felt, as one of them wrote, that their multicultural agencies (MCAs) were

"Only focused on Hispanic market with same/similar messaging as general market and not truly differentiated to meet the true needs of this target."

Moreover, clients are frustrated that they have to endure multiple and seemingly redundant meetings and billings to solve a single problem: how to build the brand. And that effort isn't always translating into the proper execution. Consider that brands have responded to the Hispanic market's tremendous growth by shifting more of their budgets to focus on that audience. That's an entirely rational approach, given that population's escalation. Growth in ad spending of 8 percent, as you can see in the following chart from eMarketer (Figure 3.1), is awfully healthy, especially when it's compared against the growth in overall media spending, which stood at just over 5 percent in 2014.

	2012	2013	% change
TV	**$5,794**	**$6,102**	**5.3%**
—Network TV	$4,206	$4,618	9.8%
—Spot TV	$1,323	$1,269	-5.5%
—Cable TV	$246	$215	-12.4%
Print	**$1,016**	**$1,153**	**13.5%**
—Newspapers	$683	$779	14.1%
—Magazines	$294	$333	13.3%
—Other print	$39	$40	2.6%
Internet*	**$440**	**$580**	**31.8%**
Spot radio	**$431**	**$466**	**8.0%**
Total	$7,681	$8,301	8.1%

Note: numbers may not add up to total due to rounding; *Ad Age DataCenter estimates
Source: Advertising Age with Kantar Media, Latino Print Network and Nielsen, "Hispanic Fact Pack: Annual Guide to Hispanic Marketing and Media 2014 Edition," July 29, 2014

179795   www.e**Marketer**.com

FIGURE 3.1   U.S. Hispanic Ad Spending, by Media, 2012 and 2013: Millions and Percent Change

Source: Advertising Age and Kantar Media "Hispanic Fact Pack," 2014.

(Incidentally, the most interesting part of this chart is the growth in Internet spending. Nearly 32 percent! As you'll learn later, U.S. Hispanics are huge consumers of digital data on their phones. Marketers are getting the message.)

But the story breaks down once we factor in the black community. Although this population isn't rising as quickly as the Hispanic one, it is certainly growing considerably faster than the white population. Despite that, advertising targeted to blacks has declined, especially as general market shops have attempted to wrap blacks into the general market mantle. As Spike Lee, a 2015 inductee in the Advertising Hall of Fame, put it, "As a whole, the advertising agencies have not gotten it."

In other words, the dollars flowing toward Hispanic advertising aren't coming out of *general* market coffers. They're coming from other *multicultural* advertising pools. And it isn't a question of just shifting a few dollars here or there. The current agency model isn't flexible enough to address that problem.

In theory, GMAs speak to nearly 70 percent of the marketplace, and MCAs cover the remaining 30 percent. Clients reach only part of their audience, and advertisers and marketers fall short of their benchmarks.

Given the dissatisfaction with—and obvious shortcomings of—the current model, it's difficult to fathom how the old ways have continued to endure. There are valid reasons for the longevity of the status quo: Many GMAs have limited experience and skill in the multicultural space, and each type of agency naturally tends to feel protective of its own position. Fixing this is a matter of moving whole chunks of business from one incumbent agency to another operation—perhaps one with no long-term status with the brand. It requires pulling money away from one part of the brand's marketing organization and awarding it to another—a move that goes against established power structures, business models, and relationships.

Although that's not an easy battle to fight, the overwhelming market opportunity has made the stakes abundantly clear. A new general market is forcing change in the advertising world. We are in the midst of one of the largest shifts in population and purchasing behavior in our nation's history. It's time to adapt.

Globally, altered demographics created by burgeoning populations of youths, of members of religions outside the Judeo-Christian tradition, and of women have challenged established structures. As we mentioned earlier, the changes in the United States are just as compelling. According to 2010 census data, the U.S. population looks remarkably different than it did 30 years ago.

The total market here includes the Hispanic, black, Asian American, and LGBT audiences. Together, they make up a combined purchasing demographic superpower that now constitutes more than 40 percent of the population. As you can see from Figure 3.2, by 2010, the combined minority segments (excluding LGBT individuals) already made up 35 percent of the population.

It is important to understand not only the demographic changes but also where those changes have taken place. Figure 3.3 contains a look at how the demographics have changed

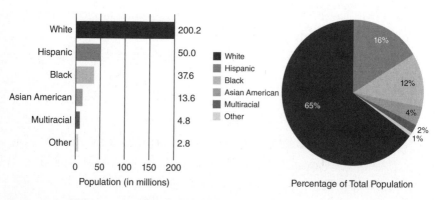

FIGURE 3.2   U.S. race and ethnicity

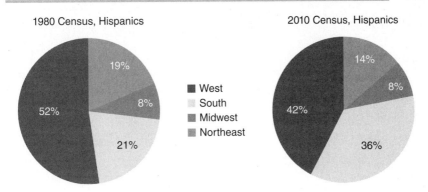

1980 Census, Hispanics

2010 Census, Hispanics

FIGURE 3.3   Geographic distribution of U.S. Hispanic population

in the United States since the 1980 census was completed. As you can see from this figure, the real growth in the Hispanic population is in the South. Fully 9 percent of all U.S. Hispanics live in Los Angeles County, and 71 percent of all U.S. Hispanics are clustered in just 100 counties nationwide. See why understanding local and regional demographics is so crucial?

Also, starting with that 1980 census, Hispanics began to post record population gains. According the U.S. Census Bureau, the Hispanic population grew from 14.6 million people in 1980 to 52 million as of 2011. Growth in the black community has been less dramatic, but that market has shifted in terms of geographic density as seen in Figure 3.4.

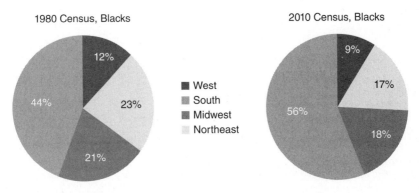

1980 Census, Blacks

2010 Census, Blacks

FIGURE 3.4   Geographic distribution of U.S. black population

Rank	State	% Hispanic	% Black	% Asian American	% Majority Minority
1	CA	38	6	13	56
2	TX	38	12	4	53
3	NY	18	14	7	39
4	FL	23	15	2	40
5	IL	16	14	5	35
6	PA	6	11	9	19
7	OH	3	12	2	17
8	MI	4	14	2	21
9	GA	9	30	9	42
10	NC	8	21	2	32

FIGURE **3.5**   2010 Census, top 10 states

When we break it down even further, we see that the results are enlightening. More than 50 percent of the people now living in California and Texas are firmly in the minority majority, as you can see in Figure 3.5. These are our two largest states in terms of population, and we cannot underestimate their impact on elections, retail, and education, as well as on media and advertising spend—as the 2016 election cycle makes clear. Immigration is a massive issue and, as in 2008 and 2012, the Hispanic vote is seen as crucial to any national candidate's chance for victory.

Marketers are curious about statewide demographics—but we are absolutely *obsessed* with metropolitan areas, because that's the level at which the real marketing spend decisions are made. In America's top 10 most populous cities, as Figure 3.6 indicates, the combined populations of Hispanics, blacks, and Asian Americans account for at least 50 percent of a city's total population. Majority

Rank	City	State	% Hispanic	% Black	% Asian American	% Majority Minority
1	New York	NY	29	23	13	64
2	Los Angeles	CA	49	9	11	69
3	Chicago	IL	29	32	5	67
4	Houston	TX	44	23	6	73
5	Philadelphia	PA	12	42	6	61
6	Phoenix	AZ	41	6	3	50
7	San Antonio	TX	63	6	2	72
8	San Diego	CA	29	6	16	51
9	Dallas	TX	42	25	3	70
10	San Jose	CA	33	3	32	68

FIGURE **3.6**   2010 Census, top U.S. cities

minority populations account for more than 60 percent of the population in five of these cities, and in three—Houston, San Antonio, and Dallas—it comprises 70 percent or more of the residents.

These massive changes are no surprise; anyone paying attention to demographic shifts has seen them coming. It's the speed with which they have occurred that's shocking. Most predictions estimated our population wouldn't look like it does now until 2050.

And demographics are just one piece of this puzzle. Businesses are motivated by profit opportunities. Here, too, the majority minority shows its strength. The combined spending power of Hispanics, blacks, Asian Americans, and multiracial American communities is larger than the gross domestic product of many global markets, such as Brazil, India, Spain, Russia, Australia, and Argentina.

Per household, the majority minority outspent what's considered the general market today in most categories (see Figure 3.7). Although this makes sense once you think about it—all of the so-called minorities combined now add up to a majority—the market's sheer *size* is sobering. Just look at transportation

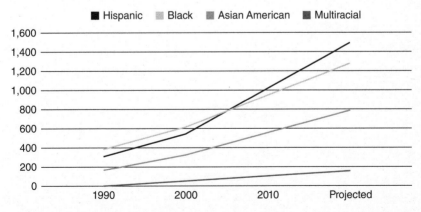

FIGURE **3.7** Multicultural buying power 1990–2015 (in billions of dollars)

Categories	White	Majority Minority	Difference
Transportation	8,172	21,242	13,070
Food	5,488	18,183	12,695
Insurance & Pensions	4,247	14,897	10,650
Apparel	1,642	5,907	4,265
Healthcare	2,588	5,829	3,241
Entertainment	2,220	5,338	3,118
Education	791	3,625	2,834
Personal Care Products	536	1,625	1,089
Furniture	427	906	479
Alcohol	425	818	393
Laundry & Cleaning Supplies	133	448	315

FIGURE **3.8**   U.S. Average Annual Expenditure Spending: White versus Black, Hispanic, and Asian American (in Dollars)

spending. The majority minority spends more than two and a half times what whites spend. The trend continues all the way down the line, with majority minority consumers spending more on everything from food to furniture (see Figure 3.8).

Big Market, Big Opportunity, and Big Confusion

The gulf between the incredible spending power of the majority minority market and the resources devoted to capturing it has frustrated me. As I explained in Chapter 1, that's what drove me to leave the brand world and start working at an agency. The same frustration boiled over in 2010, when I finally realized that the general market/multicultural market way of looking at the world was fundamentally flawed. I decided to speak out, and I did it by taking my fight to those who had the most to lose by ignoring what I am proposing.

In 2010, while launching the industry's first Cross-Cultural Practice, I spoke at the annual Association of National Advertisers (ANA) Multicultural Conference and advocated for a Total Market approach, first announced all those decades ago by McKinsey, pointing out that the current business model was unsuited to a majority minority world.

I challenged the entire marketing and communications industry, especially the general-market agency (GMA) world. As I said at the time, "America is at a cultural crossroads. Within the marketing and advertising circles, we are at the boiling point. You can feel the tension in all the halls of Fortune 500 companies. They're worried about the New Marketplace. There are predictions that by 2040, what's now referred to today as minorities and underserved consumers, will be what's now called the majority. This has huge macroeconomic implications in everything we do from the products we develop to the programming and media consumption we depend on."

After that talk at the ANA Multicultural Conference, Walmart announced all growth will come from the multicultural consumer.[2] Brand after brand indicated that they would be following a Total Market approach in the future.

Intentions are one thing. *Actually* altering the way a massive brand goes to market is something very different indeed. The well-intentioned brands all realized that this change would be tougher than they'd thought. After some initial attempts to become a Total Market organization, many began to grasp that this was not a marketing question—although it began there. It was a *total enterprise transformation* that would take a great deal of effort. As a result, some retreated or applied claims that the approach did not work. The Total Market approach is less about advertising and more about organizational change and education.

In 1910, a number of brands came together to form the ANA to provide "leadership that advances marketing excellence and shapes the future of the industry," as the organization's website proclaims.[3] The organization counts "more than 640 companies with 10,000 brands that collectively spend over $250 billion in marketing advertising." They're an impressive bunch.

But it was not until 1999 that the ANA formed its first multicultural conference dedicated to providing brands and businesses with best practices and standards for the separate but equal multicultural industry vertical.

Unfortunately, it was too late by then. Marketing and communications was a mature category. The incumbent business structures led general market agencies to prioritize the old qualities of the marketplace that was once white, while underfunded multicultural shops took care of the rest.

Even a cursory glance at the demographics we discussed earlier in this chapter makes clear that a marketing and communications industry set up in that way could speak to *at most* 70 percent of the population. The other 30 percent were addressed with only the crumbs off the table. Moreover, the general market approach develops its insights from attitude- and behavior-based research techniques developed in the 1930s. Though they evolved over the years, they're still based on the sample size of the so-called general market. Researchers for big brands used to hold focus groups and develop phone or mail surveys. Now they do it online. Sometimes, big brands buy third-party data from research houses, many of which have origins in the United Kingdom. Unsurprisingly, they were late to introduce multicultural marketing affiliates or provide resources for brands and businesses to use for research.

As a result, brands that relied heavily on general market research used databases that reflected only the majority population. These sources, therefore, did not reflect the trends, behaviors, and attitudes of the emerging majority minority.

Of course, general market research providers were efficient and cost-effective. The data and insights were housed in databases collected over time, and access was easy. It easily provided advertisers and researchers insights they could recommend to brands with a high degree of confidence, and it was sufficiently representative—that is, until recently.

But general market research did not characterize the *total addressable market*. Some agencies just blindly applied their findings to the total marketplace without regard for nuances in individual segments. Some couched this in language, such as *universal truth*, without ever really knowing what a representative sample size of underserved consumer segments would feel.

General market agencies were hamstrung by this blindness, even if they were unaware of it. However, multicultural agencies were equally blinkered—perhaps more so. Because of the revenue disparity, these agencies had to develop creative and business strategies without primary research. They were asked to provide their view or perspective with little access to accurate data.

Don't get me wrong: This can work in the hands of a very talented team, but even then it is sometimes a matter of creative serendipity or even luck. I recall a salient example from back in 1999, when I was working at the Miller Brewing Company. The chief marketing officer (CMO) at the time wanted to put forward a social responsibility effort centered on reducing drunk driving. At the time, I was leading multicultural marketing there, and one of my agencies was Don Coleman Associates (now known as Global Hue). Miller's CMO briefed this campaign out to the general market shop, but Don wanted to get in on it. I couldn't blame him because it was going to be a nice new piece of business. Miller paid the GMA to field the research necessary to come up with the new campaign. Don didn't have the same research tools available, and even if he'd been paid to research, he wouldn't have been able to come up with the same kinds of findings. The CMO still gave him a shot, but he told Don that he was going to have to invest in new tools.

Don's agency was (and is) absolutely stacked with talent, and they came back with an insight that I could tell wasn't founded on anything other than an ad hoc survey of a few guys in the office.

In fact, the research was so thin that I can't really call what they came back with an "insight." Instead, it was an inspiration. And it was a good one. Don's group showed us a film they'd created that wasn't about driving drunk. It was about living responsibly. Miller loved it, and we went with it. In the process, we inaugurated a new way to communicate a big social idea—via a holistic appeal to people's better natures rather than a hectoring scolding delivered over the airwaves.

The new idea worked, and I'm delighted I got to be a part of it. But I'm under no illusions about what happened. Don Coleman Associates got thrown a bone by Miller, and they turned it into a magnificent meal because of innate talent and no small amount of luck. That's great when it works, but it's hardly something business can count on.

Multicultural research methodologies did not truly evolve until the 1950s and 1960s. Brands asked multicultural vendors to use lower-cost desk research or primary research within their office or were occasionally open to funding third-party subscription services because of their lower budgets. But when the multicultural extensions from the big research houses were finally developed, they were out of reach. The cost for access was more than $20,000 annually.

A multicultural vendor going after black consumers *or* Hispanic consumers *or* Asian consumers couldn't justify that cost. The cost made sense—and even was reasonable—only in light of the three ethnic markets considered as a group.

Multicultural agencies had to improvise. They used their own research, which produced deep, ethnic-specific research findings, but without scalable or transferable data. It was a one-off solution.

Because brands were not investing appropriately in multicultural research, they relied heavily on borrowing equity from talent or sports and entertainment figures. For U.S. Hispanics, brands just adopted the general-market consumer insight and translated the creative, often changing the casting and setting.

Brands never saw the results of effective storytelling because there was little investment in true storytelling. They rarely achieved an authentic connection with ethnic customers. Instead, they just depended on borrowed relationships from figures that had already developed a relationship with multicultural consumers.

In sum, the incumbent general market/multicultural market split does not work anymore. The population has changed. The market has grown. The insights aren't good enough. The connection is insufficient.

And, most important, *consumers neither think nor behave according to the segmented approach brands and advertisers use.*

If we maintain the existing business structure, we will undermine talent development, marketplace growth and effectiveness, creative progress, company culture, and procurement.

Change, although wrenching, will be lucrative. We're witnessing the emergence of new tools and new techniques (we'll discuss them in later chapters) that address the Total Market. These will give companies the opportunity to reevaluate their brands, organization structures, offerings, products, and services. They will be able to build new experiences and drive deeper engagement with consumers. By looking through a Total Market lens, companies can finally make proper investments, setting aside underfunded decisions and inauthentic consumer connections. In short, they'll make more money, more efficiently.

We will use the next couple of chapters to share "Tales from the Front: Companies Trying to Get It Right" and "Experimenting with the Total Market Approach." Most brands and businesses continue to struggle within the emerging Total Market—even the ones we're highlighting. But they are starting to get it right, and we'll show you how they're doing it.

Chapter 4

Tales from the Front

Companies Trying to Get It Right

A dvertising sits at the center of many of the stories we've told so far, and will figure prominently in several more. Nevertheless, this is not an advertising book. Changing the advertising industry will not magically render brands fit to compete in the Total Market; however, the realization that brands must change the way they go to market is starting to flow upstream to the enterprise itself.

This is in keeping with a larger trend. Advertising and marketing has long held an unusual position in the world of business. Specifically, in a world of exact knowledge, advertising has always been woefully imprecise. As retail pioneer John Wanamaker is purported to have said, "Half the money I spend on advertising is wasted; the trouble is I don't know which half." That didn't sit any better with executives in Wanamaker's day than it does with corporate bosses today. Other enterprise functions don't suffer from this problem. The costs of goods, staff, rent, and so on—these are all known to a penny, as is revenue. Every well-run business knows exactly how much money is coming in the door through sales and licensing. And profit—the difference between the revenue coming in and the costs going out—grows when a business increases revenue or shrinks costs.

Brand is the mechanism by which businesses establish a consumer preference for a product. As my former Ogilvy & Mather colleague Joanna Seddon wrote in "The Brand in the Boardroom," "Brand establishes a nonrational hold over the behavior of the stakeholder, which leads them to prefer the company's offer to competitors'. This creates a co-relationship between the stakeholder and the company, guaranteeing a flow of future sales and profits."[1] Companies have long known about the power of the brand, but vague measurement hampered their efforts to cultivate it. Seddon and others did pioneering work on valuing brands, and that, combined with the surge in reliable data the digital revolution enabled, gave companies the ability to begin assessing the real impact of brands and marketing.

This put brand stewardship on an equal footing with financial stewardship. And when you consider that the brand is often the most valuable equity any company has, it's amazing this development has been so long in coming.

This has significant implications for the business world. Advertising and marketing cares for—and sometimes creates—a company's most valuable asset. That asset is perceived by a majority of the population as crucial to a company's success. When we change the way a company goes to market for more than half of the population, we not only change the advertising and marketing, but we also have to change the enterprise itself. Otherwise, the outcome is communications tokenism. The consumer doesn't want and can see right through that. Consumers want their brands to answer *their* needs—not the needs of the old majority. All sorts of things need to change for that to happen—suppliers, talent mix, research, distribution, sales terms, experience, identity, purpose, product attributes, customer service, and the list goes on. But the lens through which consumers will perceive all of that is the brand. This is where every transformation ends up.

Starting the Transformation

When I asked the executives at Ogilvy & Mather whether they wanted to build a business or just feel good, I was really asking them whether they wanted to help transform their *clients'* businesses. In this regard, unfortunately, the advertising industry was well behind its clients. One of the unintended outcomes of the existing separate but equal advertising system was underrepresentation of minority populations at general-market houses. Diversity and inclusion has been part of the agenda at corporate brands since the 1960s. No consumer brand could afford to ignore a sizable percentage of its customers, after all. But ad agencies had corporate brands as their customers. So not only were individuals to whom they were selling mostly white men, but they were also freed from having to think about minority populations by the presence of multicultural agencies. Accordingly, it was not until around the year 2000 that most of the large agency holding companies institutionalized the practice of diversity and inclusion.

But when they got it, they got it. Advertising agencies, after all, win or lose depending on how well they understand the consumer. They could read demographic data as well as anyone else, and they knew what it held. But there was a long distance from coming to that realization and crafting a credible offering.

I wanted the Cross-Cultural Practice to bridge that distance. You may recall from Chapter 1 that cross-cultural thinking concerns itself with the ways in which members of different cultures interact among themselves *and* with each other. Being a general-market agency (GMA) with a strong, if new, commitment to diversity and inclusion, Ogilvy & Mather had a good case to make there. We were founded over a half century ago by one of the pioneers of advertising—the man who gets credit for defining the modern concept of the brand—and we were ready to redefine the industry to meet the challenges for the next 50 years.

We kicked off the Cross-Cultural Practice in 2011 with an event attended by the original game changers and segment pioneers for multicultural advertising and media. They came into the theater in our new offices overlooking the Hudson River to hear what we had to say.

They didn't like it one bit. Less than 1 percent of Ogilvy budgets had gone to multicultural agencies over the past 12 months. So when we showed them what we were planning, they were, well, let's just call it skeptical.

Earning Credibility

Consumers are smart. As David Ogilvy said, "The consumer is not a moron. She's your wife." They know what is and is not an authentic presentation of your brand and company. Marketing professionals are *especially* savvy consumers, given what they do for a living. And the multicultural media and agency professionals in that room were not buying what we were there to sell. We offered partnership. They saw a threat. We offered scale. They saw appropriation. We offered a new way to go to market. They saw an internal culture that hadn't yet changed enough.

And it is that last point that is most significant. Let's consider the case of Wyndham Worldwide. This global hospitality company spun off from Cendant in 2006, a time when shifting demographics were already obvious. But Wyndham wasn't a conventional start-up; it was a collection of existing hospitality brands that had once been part of a travel and hospitality conglomerate. Although the underlying businesses had a long tenure, Wyndham Worldwide itself was new, which meant it had a chance to define itself for itself. Like many companies, it used the vehicle of core values—of which Wyndham has five—to do that. One of them reads, "Provide individual opportunity and accountability: As leaders, we need to actively include diversity in our thought process. Diversity or inclusion—here at Wyndham Worldwide, it is the same concept. Being inclusive expands our horizons and our society."[2] The company felt diversity was so important to its future that it highlighted this concept as one of the five things that made Wyndham what it was.

Wyndham had also inherited a large existing organization consisting of numerous properties and thousands upon thousands of employees. Although it had always been a champion of diversity, it was still an organization that reflected the old majority—not the new minority majority. It felt that transforming itself into a hospitality business fit for the coming world meant that it first needed to transform itself internally. As such, it adopted an enterprise-wide effort to diversify its workforce over three dimensions, as you can see in Figure 4.1, which categorizes different types of diversity that the workforce possesses. Wyndham doesn't consider these categories as being things to

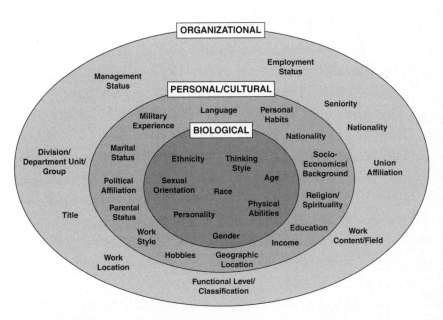

FIGURE 4.1 Different dimensions of diversity

adapt to. Instead it thinks of them as a wide-ranging group of skills and attributes that its employee base maintains.

From there, it moved outward to create business diversity and supplier diversity in addition to devoting itself to building a multicultural talent pipeline for the future. Only then did Wyndham feel that it was ready to present itself authentically to the majority minority marketplace as a true Total Market hotelier. As of this writing, Wyndham had just begun that last part of its transformation, but it's keenly aware of the need to create experiences appropriate to the expectations of the Total Market—cross-cultural experiences.

The advertising industry did not have the luxury of an orderly transition period. The old models were structurally unable to adapt to the new marketplace. The short-term financial incentives coaxed executives toward the status quo—as I found out that day in 2009 when I launched the Cross-Cultural Practice.

It was a lesson I received again a year later when I took the same message to the Association of National Advertisers (ANA) Multicultural Conference in Miami. Representatives from more than 500 brands head down to the Atlantic beaches for some schmoozing and idea exchanges in between trips to the surf and the bar. It's a typical conference at which I was a regular, having attended numerous times as a representative of the big brands I worked for.

This time, however, I was there in a very different capacity. I was going to present my vision for a Total Market approach, and do it as a member of one of the biggest general-market shops. I didn't know how the other attendees would receive me. I was a longtime colleague of many of the people down there, but this time, I had a message that potentially threatened their way of doing business.

Once again, I got the cold shoulder. Multicultural agencies saw me as a danger to their businesses. Brand representatives knew that GMAs just didn't get ethnic segments enough to market to them. Finally, Ogilvy & Mather hadn't made a careful, public transformation to being a more diverse agency.

The social shunning was just a prelude to the tepid reception to my presentation. The audience listened politely and then fervently hoped I would just go away without saying anything more.

Not only did I threaten the status quo models, but I also called their work into question (which, incidentally, is not a great way to make friends in my business). The black agencies relied on borrowed equity from major sports and entertainment figures. Music and sports celebrities have long been effective stand-ins for deeply engaging solutions to business issues. I pointed that out—and noted as well that it was just a cosmetic solution that wouldn't hold amid the demographic changes. The Asian agencies were effective, but they were siloed and largely silent. The lesbian, gay, bisexual, transgender, and questioning (LGBTQ) agencies were only starting to find their voices. I gave them both a pass, but I did point out that their isolation had to end. The Hispanic agencies were riding the wave of population growth, enjoying ballooning budgets, and feeling flush. They were interested in speaking to Hispanics and Hispanics alone.

Things were good for everyone, and here I was trying to disrupt the whole thing.

I wasn't just advocating for new business models; I was also suggesting that we rethink our cherished definitions of culture.

Let's Talk about Race

You were wondering when this would come in, weren't you? Sorry to disappoint, but this isn't the place to have a robust discussion about race. And I'm not the person to have it. I have the life experience of being a black male in America—along with millions of others. Every human of every race carries some legacy of racism. We all make assumptions about people based on ethnicity, either ours or theirs, no matter how much we try not to.

I come from Spartanburg, South Carolina. My dad was in the air force, and like everyone else in my neighborhood, I was raised by my mother. We all shared father figures with the Smith, Fowler, and Blythe families. Like a lot of kids of my generation, I grew up in the crack era, and my neighborhood—Amherst—sat right in between two housing projects: Spartanburg Terrace and Highland.

It's been a while since crack has been in the headlines, but black America is still dealing with the consequences of the epidemic that raged in the 70s, 80s, and 90s. Members of an entire generation—my generation—of black men were decimated by crack. (*Decimated* is one of those words that is thrown around a lot without much care shown for its meaning. To decimate means to kill one out of every 10—and in this case, I'm using the word accurately. One out of every 15 black men is currently incarcerated while one out of every three black men can expect to be arrested at one point or another. I figure I'm being generous by *only* calling what happened "decimation.")

Many in the crack era were looking for a little relief from a difficult life and trying financial circumstances. Jobs were rapidly disappearing, especially the good ones that paid a living wage. Social mobility seemed like a joke. The physical environment was depressing. At the same time, the larger economy was booming, and the ubiquity of mass media drove that other life— the one you could never hope to have—right into your face. Sometimes folks just wanted to escape for a while. The old script went like this: Head down to the convenience store and pick up a six-pack of beer, or hit up the local dope dealer for a dime bag. No big deal. But as times got tougher, the price of that six-pack moved out of reach. Ten or 12 bucks was too much to spend. How about a 40? That's a buck 99. Hold up. That malt liquor is six and a half percent alcohol whereas the beer is only four and a half or five. That's a pretty easy decision for the man looking to have the world go hazy for a bit. And it was the only option for a while.

And then along came crack. Sure, a couple of rocks cost 10 bucks, and that was more than you could really afford. But you just heard that it would send you to the moon, and by morning you'd be back. It was a fast trip, too. Grab a can, punch a few holes, insert the flame, watch the rock burn, and the next thing you know, you're in orbit. You know you're not going to get hooked. You're no junky. You can't afford to be. It's just this once. You just need a little escape.

Only you do get hooked. It's inevitable. It's *chemical*.

That's just one slice of the experience of growing up in America during the 1980s; there are countless other stories, better and worse. My experiences may be different from yours, but we are more similar than we are different. I cherish family, but my circle of intimates may span more generations. I want to succeed, but I may spend my money differently. I love good food, but my tastes may run to different things. I want my kids to grow up in a good neighborhood, but I may define that differently. For a brand to understand what kind of products, services, and experiences I want and how I want them marketed to me, that brand is going to have to get to know me. And that means my cultural milieu—my history, my family, my upbringing, my hopes, my frustrations, my likes and dislikes, my values, and, yes, my race—is going to have to be discussed.

Now, given what I've just told you about the world we grew up in during the 1980s, do you think that conversation is going to be easy and comfortable for a bunch of white marketing executives?

This is why we avoid the conversation—and instead outsource ethnic advertising to multicultural agencies that know their slices of the world firsthand. But their budgets, set according to one slice or another of the minority population, aren't large enough to do proper research. So they rely on the draw of celebrities to communicate their shared understanding. (Let's put Terrence Howard in the ad!) Or we substitute symbols, slang, and language for real cultural understanding. (Wait a minute . . . how about a deep-voiced black voiceover artist who says *brother* or *man?*) Want to reach Hispanics? Take the general-market word, translate it into Spanish, and then head home for the night.

That approach won't work anymore. According to the Pew Research Center, 35 percent of the 20 million second-generation immigrants in the United States are Hispanic. Overwhelmingly, they think of themselves as typical Americans. They don't need or want Spanish-language marketing, but they do expect communications to be respectful and inclusive of their cultural and ethnic experience while being general to their shared experience as Americans. A quarter of these second generation immigrants marry outside of their ethnic group, and the majority of them report good relations with other ethnic groups. These populations are already cross-cultural; deep and siloed ethnic targeting can no longer reflect their experience.

We can no longer aim for or maintain ersatz connection with Hispanics, blacks, and Asian Americans either. We are part of the cultural mainstream and don't care to be part of separate diversity marketing. Sure, Hispanic, black, and Asian agencies better understand black culture and concerns, but that doesn't reflect the heterogeneous cultural existence most of us have today. And putting a black face or two into your general market is just not going to cut it. To be blunt, the black agencies have done well because of the reluctance to talk about race. That's no longer an option.

The First Fruits

Brand managers from IKEA were down at the Miami conference looking for answers. As it happened, they were frustrated with the limitations of the dual-agency approach already. IKEA was already an Ogilvy client, but now the brand wanted us to add cross-cultural marketing—with Hispanics in mind—to the mix. Once we started to look at the market, we realized why IKEA was so keen to adopt a Total Market approach: Hispanics made up more than half of its overall sales growth opportunity. If IKEA was going to continue to grow in the United States—its second-largest market worldwide—it would need to speak to multi-cultural consumers. Its competitors—Walmart, Sears, Lowe's, Target, JCPenney—were underspending dramatically for Hispanic consumers. When they did reach them, they did it badly.

With this opportunity in mind, IKEA saw growth only through Hispanic consumers. We dug deep and found that all multi-cultural consumers in the United States were particularly interested in life improvement—a notion closely linked to home and family. Our research showed that the 22 million Hispanic women in the United States are a powerfully ambitious group. They want to better their lives while participating in their culture and heritage. They see home as an expression of traditional warmth and welcome, an opportunity to demonstrate achievement, and a sacred space dedicated to family. That wasn't so different from what we'd learned from other ethnic groups. Blacks saw home as a place of spiritual nourishment in the company of family. Asians saw home as a place that set the stage for success and gave them the platform for achieving their ambitions.

If you look beneath the differences, however, you see one theme across all ethnic categories. Hispanics, Asians, and blacks alike felt that improving their lives and improving their homes were two facets of the same project. It turns out that whites did, too.

Our project showed IKEA the $4.1 billion opportunity in the majority minority market. It was its secret to growth, and as a result of the work we did, IKEA has redesigned communications and shopper experience with the Total Market in mind.

As much of a success as the IKEA engagement was, it was also one of the first indications of the limitations of an advertising-based approach. I had already been scorched by the multicultural agencies' reactions to the launch of Ogilvy & Mather's Cross-Cultural Practice, but there were internal conflicts and missed opportunities on the IKEA project—some, unfortunately, pointed out by the client itself—that highlighted the fact that Ogilvy & Mather had not yet undergone enough internal transformation to integrate cross-cultural thinking seamlessly into its core offerings. I still had work to do.

IKEA wasn't the only early adopter. We did some work with British Airways that culminated in some of the most moving creative work—the BA "Visit Mum" film—I have ever been a part of. Look it up on the Web (it's here: https://www.youtube.com/watch?v=WPcfJuk1t8s), but grab a tissue first. I don't want to give away too much, but what purports to be an advertisement for an airline is actually an incredible story of filial love and diaspora. This was the first truly successful cross-cultural work—from insight all the way to execution—that we had done. Not only was it a creative and business success, but it established a new category as well.

That's when things started to heat up. One of the world's largest consumer packaged-goods companies asked Ogilvy & Mather to be part of a global multicultural hair care pitch. Here we were, a general-market network, competing against pure-play multicultural agencies. That alone was a big deal. We wouldn't have even been invited into that conversation a year earlier, but our internal transformation was now well under way. And it must have shown—because we won the pitch. We urged our client to step away from multicultural habits and rethink the entire category. Instead of *ethnic* hair care, we asked it to reconsider the way hair care should be sold in a Total Market environment. Our solution was to view the category in terms of hair texture. It was the right idea, but it was the wrong time. This global client recognized that going from selling based on ethnicity to marketing based on texture would have worldwide implications for its product lines. Some traditionally general-market brands would have to sell to multicultural consumers while ethnic brands would need to broaden their appeal. This time Ogilvy & Mather was ready to lead this cross-cultural communications effort, but our client had not yet arrived at the right point in its internal evolution. The engagement devolved into a more traditional ethnic hair campaign.

The multicultural-brand manager from a global beverage giant saw my speech at the ANA conference, and she recognized that her company needed to hear this message as well. She convened a one-day training session to get cross-cultural thinking percolating inside the company and asked me to be a part of it. Although it was a remarkable day, the impact was limited because the company didn't follow the training with internal organizational and cultural change. It set no expectations or goals other than the maddeningly vague "awareness building." Predictably, little changed, and three years after that session, the ads from that company are not cross-cultural in any way. They are just cosmetically diverse.

My speech at the 2010 ANA conference was the start of a general shift toward Total Market thinking. At the 2011 edition of the conference, Walmart announced that it was going to "blow up" its multicultural-marketing budget and simply move the money into the business units. A year later, Walmart's Tony Rogers announced that "One hundred percent of the growth [in sales] is going to come from multicultural customers."

I felt the momentum building. We heard from other big brands. By this point, we knew that Total Market thinking required us to focus on more than just advertising. We understood at last that the agency and the client needed to work together to make the whole business into a Total Market Enterprise (to learn more about this model, see Chapter 5). And with a global infant and child care brand, we finally got our chance. For brands like that, the transition to the majority minority isn't off in the future. It's happening right now. As of this writing, 51 percent of babies born in the United States are in the minority majority. To remain a market leader, that brand had to become a Total Market organization fast while using the cross-cultural approach. Everyone from the retailers to the brand mangers knew that they needed to change, but large enterprises don't turn fast. Our ideas kept making their way to the very top of the company only to get shot down at the last moment. The campaign ended up being strong Hispanic-focused work without enough cross-cultural insight to be as effective as we'd hoped.

That said, the experience provided the aha moment I needed. I was never going to usher in Total Market thinking through advertising and marketing; the inertia was too strong. The fits and stumbles led me to realize that all the players were fixated on updating advertising to meet the needs of the Total Market. The real change for brands and agencies alike needed to come at the level of the whole organization. We didn't need better advertising outcomes. We needed a strategic organizational shift. Communications engagements couldn't achieve that kind of change. I needed a better lever.

That lever was enterprise education. If I was going to help companies reach the Total Market, I needed to help them transform into Total Market Enterprises.

I'll show you how to become one.

Chapter 5

Experimenting with the Total Market Approach

I moved to New York in 2008 after working down in Austin, Texas. Life was good down south; my family and I loved the weather, our home, and our community. But much as we loved it, we decided that we needed to make our own version of a great northern migration—and headed to New York. Just as it was a generation before, that's where the jobs were—specifically for me, where the agencies were.

After practicing and building the cross-cultural approach, I saw a larger opportunity beyond marketing and at the enterprise level. For brands and businesses, the Total Market transformation had to happen at the enterprise level, and I knew I had to make another big shift. Not out of New York—but out of advertising altogether. I took a deep breath and jumped, forming a new company called REFRAME: The Brand in 2014 dedicated to teaching individuals, brands, and enterprises how to adapt to the new marketplace. I told my wife, only partially in jest, that I had finally made it off the plantation.

This chapter will give you an overview of the Total Market Enterprise approach. It's the same program that my new company sells to major global brands interested in becoming New Majority ready using the Total Market Enterprise approach. Following this introduction, we'll go through each of the five key steps for your Total Market Enterprise transformation.

What Is the Total Market Enterprise Approach?

You can develop a Total Market approach using your current staff and vendors, presuming your organization has been generally adhering to diversity guidelines. But just because you have people of color in your organization along with healthy lesbian, gay, bisexual, and transgender (LGBT) representation doesn't mean you're good to go. You likely still need to undertake major internal and external transformations.

As I pointed out in the last chapter, insufficient preparation for the Total Market can torpedo even the best-intentioned efforts to make your organization ready for the minority majority population. Not every enterprise will need to adopt the Wyndham model.

Diversity and inclusion doesn't have to be a core value. Your enterprise may have different, equally worthy values that have nothing to do with staff makeup. But you can't ignore the issue altogether, either. We're stuck with the word *diversity* because it's the one that everybody understands, but I think it's mealy mouthed. This isn't about diversity anymore. It's about *accuracy* or *representativeness*.

You'd be a damned fool not to have your workforce accurately reflect your consumer base nowadays. And although you may not be there yet, if your organization isn't at least making good strides in this direction, stop reading right now, and go yell at your human resources department. Ignoring representative hiring isn't just wrong; it's stupid.

Wyndham took a very sequential approach. It diversified its employee and supplier base first and then made sure that leadership positions fell to a representative population as well. Only *then* did the company feel ready to tackle the New Majority using the Total Market Enterprise approach. Other companies can do this all in parallel, but however you do it, the good news is that you can do it at every level of your organization, from office to department to enterprise, and that the process is relatively straightforward.

As you know already, 80 percent of U.S. growth is projected to come from the minority majority, but the business and marketing models for reaching them have gone unchanged since the 1960s. That wasn't just a different era demographically; it was a different time technologically as well. In fact, the changes we're seeing in our population mimic the changes that the digital revolution has wrought. Until the 1990s, you could reliably reach the vast majority of the population by advertising on one of the big three networks. Major TV events, such as the Super Bowl, still draw huge numbers of people, but consider that last year's Super Bowl, often cited as the most popular U.S. broadcast in history, was essentially a tie with the finale of *M*A*S*H* back in 1983—despite the population being nearly one-third smaller back then. That episode was watched by two-thirds of U.S. households.

That was probably the last time ever that two-thirds of America did the same thing at the same time. By the time *M*A*S*H*'s "Goodbye, Farewell and Amen" rolled credits, America's demographic changes were already well under way. The nation would never again be as homogeneous as it had been then.

Immigration and birth rates weren't the only things dismantling the old order. The technological revolution was to be just as profound a disruption. Oceans of ink—both real and virtual— have been spilled over the changes the digital age have brought to the way we live, and there's no need to add much to that pool. Let me remind you, however, of an early digital worry.

At the dawn of the broadband era, digital access was unevenly distributed. Getting online was an expensive business, requiring pricy hardware and services. Broadband access was often unavailable in predominantly minority areas. As a result, minority populations had sharply lower rates of Internet penetration. The smartphone changed all of that by opening up digital connectivity to all. Not only did Internet access rates even out, but digital energy and innovation also shifted toward the burgeoning minority population. That makes sense when you think about it. There was pent-up demand, and the population skewed younger.

Digital access brought about an even more profound cultural fragmentation than the simultaneous demographic changes going on. Every subculture could now find its home on the net. The barriers to broad-scale self-expression—market access and distribution—were erased in an instant, and as a result, culture went from being the shared consumption of a social common denominator to a heterogeneous mix that individuals customized and added to at their discretion.

I'll leave it to the sociologists to analyze, but from a marketer's perspective, the important change is this: We became cross-cultural. What we used to call multicultural became simply *culture*—because every culture has equal access to our eyes and ears. Cross-cultural appreciation means understanding individual cultures and the ways in which they interact and trade social DNA. Practical considerations of appropriate spending, market size, and so on aside, that right there is the reason why businesses must adopt a Total Market approach. We are a cross-cultural society. We can no longer sell to any one group without grappling with the ways in which that group has been influenced and changed by all the others.

A New Industry Vertical

Let's get down to the nitty-gritty. The Total Market approach creates a new industry vertical. As you may or may not know, all business functions—from finance to digital marketing—are people in the business of servicing needs. A purchasing department hires the people who service those needs and classifies those providers as *horizontal* businesses. Horizontal businesses receive revenue dollars for the service or product they provide to the company. A duct tape company's finance division or its sales department is an example of a horizontal business. Depending on how big the companies are that provide the product or service, they have to report earnings or revenue. And that business's designation is listed within an industry vertical so that analysts can track and report growth against other industry competitors. The industry vertical is the market to which the company is unifying its horizontal offerings to sell to. In other words, the market for duct tape.

Before I reintroduced the Total Market approach, the $300 billion marketing and communications industry was divided into two big verticals: general market and multicultural market. The Total Market approach suggests that we dispense with those two market verticals and instead reorganize our businesses according to a new one—the Total Market. See Figure 5.1.

Some major restructuring of business must occur to make this happen. Nearly every major corporation has a diversity function of some sort or another. That's probably joined by a

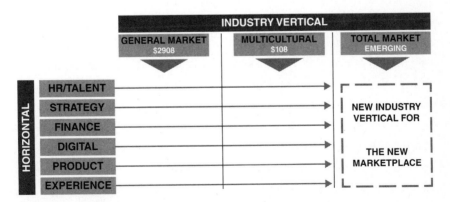

FIGURE 5.1   A new industry vertical

multicultural-marketing division as well as general-market media, agencies, and communications. All of that needs to go. I'm not criticizing those functions. They were crucial steps for business to take, especially when minority populations were still so much smaller than the white majority. But now that we're a plurality nation, those former divisions aren't just outdated; they're obstacles to growth. Companies will need to become Total Market Enterprises, characterized by the following traits:

- They reframe their industries' and brands' approach to the total addressable market.
- They fully invest in addressing the Total Market opportunity for brand building.
- They curate a deeper level of understanding of the new consumers.
- They develop innovation and new services according to the new industry vertical.
- They build Total Market–ready talent pools.
- They create effective Total Market experiences and brands.

For the short haul, this restructuring is going to introduce organizational complexity: the very thing that business has spent the past few decades trying to stamp out. The end result of the shift—which likely won't take place for many years—will be a simpler structure for business. Companies of the future will be organized according to marketplace needs rather than individual enterprise functions. The approach will be less about what the company does and more about what the consumers want.

Total Market Enterprises will need to focus simultaneously on cultural commonalities and distinctions. Businesses will need to see both the rocky stream and the individual pebbles, and they'll need to communicate with people in ways that recognize such dual identities in inclusive, respectful, and nuanced ways.

That's all there is to it: Total Market Enterprises are built according to cross-cultural organization principles and cross-cultural communications.

Achieving New Majority Readiness—Total Market Enterprise Maturity Model

No business, particularly a large one, can expect to transform into a Total Market Enterprise overnight. In fact, the process plays out over five stages: Total Market Enterprise levels one through five. Some industries, such as infant care, need to move swiftly through the stages to remain relevant. For others, the process can play out over a longer period. But all of them will need to retrain their employee base around four areas of mastery:

1. Market sizing (or Total Market valuation)
2. Organizational design and partnerships
3. Experience and engagements
4. Measurement

To figure out how to become a Total Market Enterprise, a business must first understand where it currently is in the process. It must assess its readiness to meet the Total Market era. In the next chapter, I'll lay out what the Total Market assessment looks like and how you can use it. Despite the tremendous variation in Total Market readiness, I've seen that businesses generally fall into one of five levels (see Figure 5.2). Moreover, enterprises generally pass through these levels in sequence on their way to becoming Total Market Enterprises.

Each stage indicates the evolution of the organization with respect to understanding and being ready for the New Majority. To grasp the organization's maturity fully, I assess it through stakeholder interviews or the Total Market Enterprise assessment

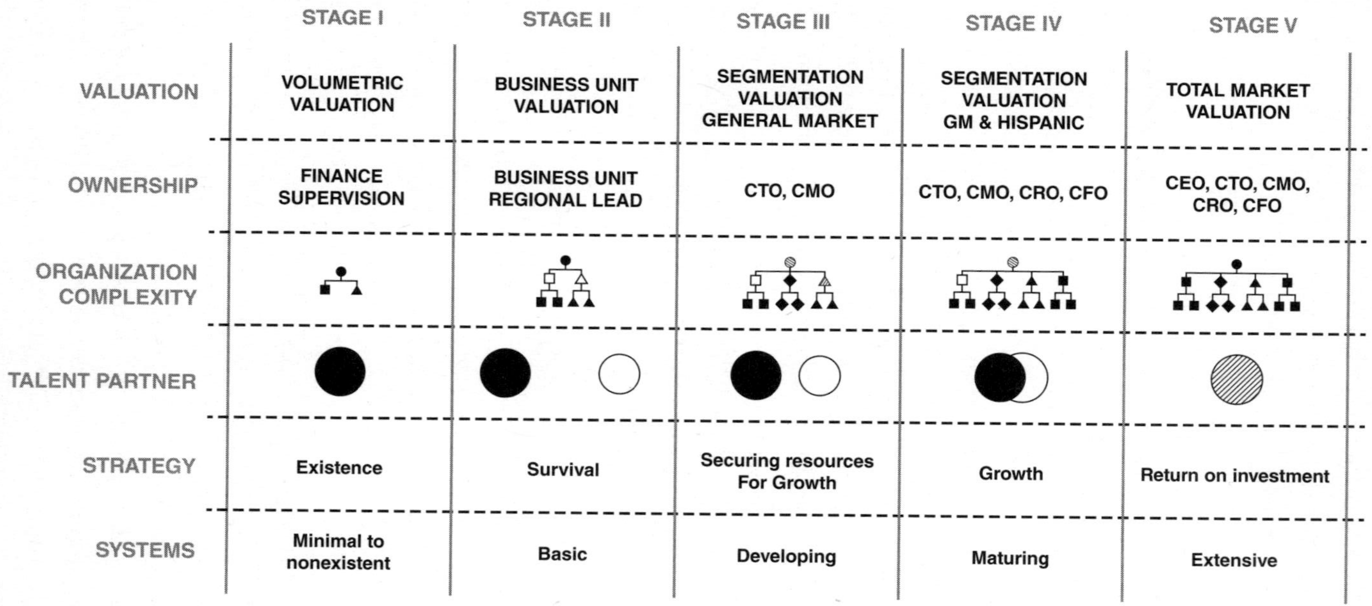

	STAGE I	STAGE II	STAGE III	STAGE IV	STAGE V
VALUATION	VOLUMETRIC VALUATION	BUSINESS UNIT VALUATION	SEGMENTATION VALUATION GENERAL MARKET	SEGMENTATION VALUATION GM & HISPANIC	TOTAL MARKET VALUATION
OWNERSHIP	FINANCE SUPERVISION	BUSINESS UNIT REGIONAL LEAD	CTO, CMO	CTO, CMO, CRO, CFO	CEO, CTO, CMO, CRO, CFO
ORGANIZATION COMPLEXITY					
TALENT PARTNER					
STRATEGY	Existence	Survival	Securing resources For Growth	Growth	Return on investment
SYSTEMS	Minimal to nonexistent	Basic	Developing	Maturing	Extensive

FIGURE 5.2   The five levels of Total Market readiness

Note: CTO stands for chief technology officer, CMO for chief marketing officer, CRO for customer revenue officer, and CFO for chief financial officer.

70

tool, which I'll introduce you to in the next chapter. Most organizations I've worked with usually fall between stages one through three.

If you look at Figure 5.2, you'll see six horizontal categories. Let's go through them in order from top to bottom.

The goal of this whole process is to understand how an organization perceives the marketplace opportunity, also known as the valuation. Is it sizing the opportunity appropriately? It is doing so across the organization? And is it ascribing proper meaning or value to it?

The second step is to understand ownership within the enterprise organization. Depending on the size of the valuation of the total addressable market (and the message the organization wants to send to investors about growth) ownership can sit in finance, a business unit lead, or someone from the C-suite.

Next we consider where barriers are within the organization and the complexity such barriers introduce. Given the shift required, we have to understand what parts of the enterprise require the most education, training, or influence in bringing this new approach to the organization.

Fourth, we look at the functional talent management group (including general, compensation, diversity, and inclusion). It's usually the easiest to assess and understand, because this is the group with the best appreciation of the business case for internal diversity. However, it is sometimes difficult for it to own the marketplace requirements.

Next we evaluate the organization's strategy for pursuing the New Majority. The level of appreciation for this within corporate strategy is going to vary across organizations.

Last we look at systems. If an organization were to get the Total Market approach up and running as well as embraced, what systems does it have to measure the impact both internally and externally? The systems can range from those that track the market opportunity to marketing automation, performance management, talent assessment, and external customer capabilities.

Let's look more deeply at development across each of the four functional areas.

Total Market Enterprise Level 1

A company at this level would answer the assessment questions like this:

Market sizing—A level 1 enterprise is still using volumetric and demographic data in making business decisions. It looks purely at the national level to understand its opportunity. It may also rely on internal shipping data. It's generally not aware of the nuances of regional- and city-level population differences.

Organizational design and partnerships—A level 1 organization is still in the very early stages from a talent perspective. Its diversity and inclusion targets are based on getting the right number and colors of bodies into the organization. It sees this as a compliance issue and, as a result, expends little energy on building a culture of inclusion. It treats partnerships the same way—as a box to check. No emphasis is placed on building cross-cultural understanding and relationships via their vendor population.

Experience and engagements—Level 1 enterprises have no culturally driven experience and engagement initiatives. Instead, they are based on sales patters and trade sales requirements. Any insight and research about Total Market populations is siloed because of the absence of organizational pathways and feedback opportunities.

Measurement—An organization at this stage has no performance and talent development process, automated or manual, built on Total Market measures. Business lines and employees alike are not measured against success in the Total Market. The chief technology officer, chief information officer, and chief marketing officer have no formal connections; in fact, they are rival colleagues with turfs to protect.

TOTAL MARKET ENTERPRISE LEVEL 2

A company at this level would answer these assessment questions like this:

Market sizing—Level 2 companies are still using volumetric and product data but have started to look at national and regional measures.

Organizational design and partnerships—This level of enterprise has realized that diversity and inclusion has business value. As a result, it realizes that diverse talent and vendor strategies are a valuable way to drive competitive advantage. This organization probably has both a chief talent officer and a chief diversity officer.

Experience and engagements—Although a level 2 company is on its way to the Total Market internally, the external perception has not yet caught up because internal developments haven't resulted in any changes in the way the company goes to market. The internal mission and purpose of the enterprise are out of alignment with consumer expectations of it.

Measurement—Companies like this have technology in place to obtain and analyze rich customer data, but these programs and platforms are siloed and unconnected to regional market and outcome analysis. They have little, perhaps no, data about talent development according to Total Market metrics and no sense of how their talent strategies affect regional market success.

TOTAL MARKET ENTERPRISE LEVEL 3

A company at this level would answer the assessment questions like this:

Market sizing—Level 3 enterprises still use volumetric data—this time at the national, regional, and local levels. They add value-based segmentations to their data, but sample size calculation generally does not account for underserved and minority majority audiences.

Organizational design and partnerships—Chief talent and chief diversity officers in level 3 organizations partner closely. They build strategy and measure talent and partnerships against minority majority outcomes at the enterprise level. Talent and diversity functions move up higher in the organization, with both functions now reporting to the president or CEO.

Experience and engagements—Level 3 companies have a customer value proposition (a internal statement written from the consumer's perspective articulating why the customer should buy the company's product or service) that includes all customer segments and takes into account every place the company and customer interact, from communications through call centers.

Measurement—Enterprises at this stage now have internal systems in place to measure performance against Total Market metrics. They also collect external data from credible sources, such as their customers and industry measures. However, they have not yet integrated those data streams, and they have no change-oriented feedback loop in place.

TOTAL MARKET ENTERPRISE LEVEL 4

A company at this level would answer the assessment questions like this:

Market sizing—Although level 4 enterprises have completed their Total Market segmentations to augment national and regional data, they are skewing their emphasis toward high-growth segments (such as U.S. Hispanics) and failing to integrate the rest of the Total Market opportunity in a holistic fashion.

Organizational design and partnerships—Chief talent officer and chief diversity officer move in lockstep in level 4 companies. They both understand how talent and vendor relationships drive growth. As a result, performance of talent and supplier pools at the enterprise and individual level is assessed according to the growth they drive.

Experience and engagements—Level 4 companies deliver Total Market experiences through every practice area in the organization, via suppliers, and externally to the customer base.

Measurement—Internal systems in level 4 enterprises are tied to the customer value proposition, are shared with customers, and harken back to plans for performance. Customer and employee satisfaction surveys align with the customer value proposition.

TOTAL MARKET ENTERPRISE LEVEL 5

A company at this level would answer the assessment questions like this:

Market sizing—Level 5 companies have achieved Total Market mastery. They have completed segmentation for every audience segment, with accurate and representative measures for all demographic targets: Hispanic, black, Asian, LGBT, and so on.

Organizational design and partnerships—Enterprises at level 5 are quite similar to those at level 4 with the addition of a reward and compensation structure tied to business outcomes.

Experience and engagements—Level 5 enterprises provide varied and nuanced Total Market experiences that are continually assessed via an external feedback loop. Ratings and reviews are shared in real time throughout the organization via a dashboard.

Measurement—Level 5 companies add greater integration to the capabilities they had when they were at level 4. Customer basket data, for example, can be analyzed instantly according to customer segmentation.

Some enterprises will achieve Total Market mastery in only four stages; some may find that they are imperfect reflections of one stage or another. Every company is unique, of course, but I have found these general stages to be true of most organizational evolutions.

Now that you understand the basic outlines of the changes in store for your company, it's time to learn how to assess your organization. That's the goal of our next chapter.

Chapter 6

Step One: New Majority Readiness

The Organization Assessment

If you think back to the experiences I shared with you in Chapter 4, you'll probably notice a theme: In every case, the engagement's eventual success was limited by one or another aspect of the organization's unpreparedness for the Total Market. I had to learn that by doing it, but the process I underwent led me to develop a Total Market Enterprise organization assessment. The five levels of Total Market readiness are helpful only if you can assess which stage your company is at—because that's the only way to know what to concentrate on first.

As you're already aware, becoming a Total Market Enterprise is a major disruption. So, you'd be justified in wondering why the necessary changes can't just evolve from existing diversity and inclusion programs. In the next section, I'll explain why the old ways won't work anymore.

History of Diversity and Inclusion as a Model for the Marketplace

THE COMPLIANCE ERA

Diversity programs began in the 1960s in response to civil rights inequities within the workplace. They were motivated by a desire for social justice on the one hand and a recognition of the need to acknowledge modernity on the other. Let's give our forebearers the benefit of the doubt and say that their primary goal was to demonstrate social responsibility while giving equal consideration to all employees.

Diversity programs initially took the form of collective associations and sets of resources designed to provide diverse employees a chance to demonstrate their identity within the monocultural American corporation. By the 1980s and 1990s, external trade associations were joined by internal diversity programs in large employers, dedicated to diversifying the workforce. Benefit of the doubt aside, the real goal was to make sure Jesse Jackson or Al Sharpton didn't choose to make an example of your company or industry. The 1990s were a particularly ripe time for this. Jesse Jackson took Wall Street to task in 1997 whereas Al Sharpton forced the ad business to change in 1999. At this time, companies were acting primarily out of respect for the law and fear of the activists.

The Commitment Era

Things started to move a little faster by the late 1990s. Diversity programs began to mature beyond box checking to realizing the social and business benefit of diversity and inclusion. Enterprises began to make real and measurable commitments to supplier diversity far beyond the previous generation's tokenism. A few Fortune 100 companies, including PepsiCo, Johnson & Johnson, Frito-Lay, Procter & Gamble, and General Mills, saw the coming opportunity in the growing multicultural marketplace. They stepped up their diversity and inclusion hiring and, crucially, made concerted efforts to retain and advance employees of every demographic stripe. New, diverse leadership was seen as being key to corporate success. Accelerating globalization added a new element of heterogeneity to the mix, and enterprises now set up global diversity initiatives and inclusion programs. At this point, gender diversity was still part of corporate programs.

THE COMPETITIVE ERA

About 10 years after the turn of the millennium, the 2010 census went off like a bomb in the middle of the corporate world. Companies were already reeling from the Great Recession, and the shifting demographics of their customer and employee base knocked them even further off balance. Business, being generally shrewd and highly adaptable, saw that a greater focus on diversity and inclusion initiatives could be a strategic advantage. It started to look for ways to make commercial plans that took the majority minority into account. As you know from prior chapters, this shift—going on right now—is wrenching and by no means a settled matter. Discreet diversity programs are probably on their way out in favor of an enterprise-wide partnership between business units and marketing, realigning corporate functions with the needs of a starkly different consumer and employee population in an effort to gain competitive advantage. That's the Total Market approach.

In short, the path of minorities in business and the marketplace is a journey from affirmative action leveling to market-driven competition. Is your company ready for the fight?

The Total Market Enterprise Assessment

To answer that question, an organization needs to assess its readiness for the Total Market. This assessment evaluates how the enterprise approaches and plans for the majority minority. It determines how aligned the organization's practices are to the current needs of the market for valuation, organization design, brand experience, and measurement.

The assessment itself isn't rocket science. First we assemble a wide variety of executives: C-suite; marketing, sales, and operations; sales leadership; talent and diversity and inclusion; advertising; call center; creative and research; and finance. We ask them to answer a battery of 40 questions about the organization and its Total Market readiness. The questions are grouped in six buckets designed to come up with answers to these big issues:

1. At what stage of Total Market Enterprise maturity is the organization (level 1–5)?
2. Where are the gaps within the enterprise for Total Market readiness?
3. How is the enterprise assessing the marketplace?
4. Does the organization have the right talent and structure?
5. Is the brand creating the right experiences for the new marketplace?
6. Do the right people own the transformation process?

Based on the responses, we measure whether the *enterprise*, *team*, and *individual* have solid working knowledge of the new marketplace and whether the *enterprise*, *team*, and *individuals* know what to do.

Although the assessment generally is customized to each company's needs, I've put together a nonspecific version that any enterprise can take to get a sense of where it is.

Market Valuation

1. Are you aware of your company having a consumer segmentation?
2. On a scale of 1 to 5:
   a. How knowledgeable are you about what percentage of your consumer base is the New Majority?

    b. How well do you understand the revenue goal for the next 12 months?

    c. How well do you understand the revenue goal for the next five years?

3. How much of your New Majority business accounts for your brand's overall revenue?

Organization Design and Partnership

1. Does your company have one of the following?

    a. No multicultural-marketing department

    b. A multicultural-marketing department

    c. A dedicated resource or shared service to address multicultural audiences

    d. Marketing to multicultural audiences as everyone's responsibility

    e. None of the above

2. Does your company have a diversity and inclusion resource or department?

3. If so, on a scale of 1 to 5, how effective would you say this department is in addressing marketplace needs?

4. Does your company have a policy and spend goal for minority suppliers?

5. Please read the following comments and select the response that best describes your procurement partnership program:

    a. I see the hiring of minority suppliers as compliance for hitting our procurement targets.

    b. I seek strategic partnerships with minority suppliers.

    c. I leave it up to the procurement department for hitting our minority supplier targets.

    d. I am not involved at all with the selection and partnership of minority suppliers.

e. I am not aware of our company's policy about the hiring of minority suppliers.

Experience and Engagement

On a scale of 1 to 5:

1. How would you rank your organization's ability to deliver relevant experiences and drive consumer engagement?
2. How would you rank your company's products or services in connecting with multicultural consumers?
3. How well does your company set dedicated resources (budget) aside for multicultural consumer engagement programs?
4. Within media, how reflective is your allocation of resources to the New Majority marketplace?
5. How is your retail experience geared toward the New Majority?

Measurement and Effectiveness (Internal and External)

1. Does your company have an ambition in place for capturing its fair share of the New Majority consumer base?
2. Does your company report growth within the New Majority consumer segment?
3. On a scale of 1 to 5, how well is your chief executive officer or chief finance officer prepared to discuss growth in the New Majority audience segments?
4. On a scale of 1 to 5, how well would you say your company incorporates New Majority growth within employee performance plans?
5. On a scale of 1 to 5, how integrated are New Majority growth key performance indicators incorporated in your company's dashboard (reporting)?

Five Levels to Demonstrating Total Market Enterprise Mastery

As discussed in Chapter 5, companies generally undergo five stages on their way to Total Market Enterprise mastery. This assessment places each company into one of those levels, described here from the perspective of skill sets and development rather than organizational practices. As you have, no doubt figured out, your score from 1 to 5 in the previous questions corresponds to the levels explained next. (Incidentally, these five levels do not correspond to the Total Market Enterprise stages in the previous chapter. They are just standard measures of a corporate learning curve adapted to this subject matter. For those of you particularly interested in corporate learning and development technique, this is called the capability model).

Level 1—Forming
+ New to the Total Market
+ Still learning the basics of the Total Market Enterprise approach
+ Requires guidance to perform tasks associated with Total Market
+ *Below average level of knowledge*

Level 2—Growing
+ Can perform competently tasks for the Total Market
+ Total Market skills still developing but basic performance is solid. Innovation and improvisation in the Total Market are still in the future.
+ *Average level of knowledge*

Level 3—Practicing
+ Can deal with unique situations in the execution of Total Market

- Can conduct the Total Market Enterprise approach dynamically and situationally while dealing with market and enterprise unpredictability
- *Benchmark level of knowledge*

Level 4—Leading

- Executes the Total Market approach through a practice or center of excellence designed to spread the learning throughout the enterprise
- Innovative and capable of teaching others the Total Market Enterprise approach
- *Top-tier level of knowledge*

Level 5—Mastery

- Total Market industry leader across every category
- Teaching and establishing best practices the Total Market Enterprise approach
- *Author (thought leader) or published level of knowledge*

Can You See Me Now?

What does this all look like?

It looks like Verizon.

Verizon is the largest mobile phone carrier in the United States, and it is lauded—rightly so—for having the best service in the nation. Before the 4G level, going with Verizon brought you something that none of the other networks could match: no dropped calls. Verizon's Code Division Multiple Access standard handed off calls from cell to cell with fewer problems than the competing Global System for Mobile Communications technology. The company built a reputation for bulletproof reliability even as AT&T was deluged with complaints about dropped calls in New York and San Francisco. Verizon's reputation is well earned, as my coauthor and countless others can attest, having switched from AT&T to Verizon for precisely that reason. Verizon's technical superiority has endured into the 4G era.

Despite all that, Verizon is getting its butt kicked when it comes to younger consumers, particularly in the New Majority. T-Mobile's outspoken chief executive officer, John Legere, took to television to hammer Verizon and AT&T as "dumb and dumber," largely because of their approach to millennial-targeted pricing and more diverse consumers. And the numbers back him up. In the first quarter of 2015, T-Mobile, and its similarly savvy competitor Sprint, grew at a dramatically faster pace than did Verizon or AT&T.

It's not a blip. T-Mobile and Sprint have been faster off the blocks in repositioning their enterprises to take advantage of the Total Market, and it has paid off. But Verizon is not sitting idly by. It sees where the market is going and how it needs to change to maintain a leading position. The company is embarking on the journey to become a Total Market Enterprise, and vice president of marketing—and living, breathing embodiment of the New Majority—Javier Farfan is on point.

Javier is an energetic man. He looks perpetually coiled to get up and get something—anything—done. Though he knows that meetings are an unavoidable part of corporate life, you can see that he'd rather be moving. He's happy to listen. He'd just rather take some action at the same time.

This is not the Verizon way. The company is headquartered in a massive concrete structure on a beautiful campus in Basking Ridge, New Jersey. It can be a 10-minute or longer walk from your office to the cafeteria, and as you trudge along, you'll pass conference rooms, cube farms, offices, and long, quiet halls. There is very little noise. The Verizon offices don't feel like a tech company; that energy is lacking. It feels like a solid, legacy enterprise in a mature business, which is exactly what it thought it was until demographics came along and whacked the employees on the back of their collective heads.

Javier is the result of that sharp blow. He's there to turn Verizon into a Total Market Enterprise and win, or win back, the New Majority customers it is losing. He walks around the office in sneakers and jeans while the rest of his colleagues are still in Jersey-office-park formal. His office has a TV on the wall playing music videos. It's safe to say that Javier is an unusual presence at Verizon.

He is also a living, breathing example of the New Majority. Like today's new generation of consumers, Javier grew up with a mosaic of cultural inputs influences as part of his experiential DNA. He is the child of Ecuadorian immigrants and grew up in West Harlem in New York City, which was and is a predominantly African American neighborhood. He can switch from Spanish to English at the drop of a dime, rap a Jay Z verse or a classic salsa hook, and feels just as at home in a boardroom as a night club.

Javier is also whip smart and driven, with an inborn gift for promotion. He turned that into a heterogeneous mix of academic and business success, graduating from Columbia Business School, starting a hip-hop magazine, and working for Accenture, JP Morgan Chase, Viacom, and PepsiCo. Along the way, he's ridden his gift for creativity and change management. That led him to Verizon, where he's putting all of his disparate experiences and talents to work to turn the battleship around.

Javier has responsibility for cultural engagement (formerly known as multicultural marketing) in the Verizon argot. When he walked in the doors, he found an organization set up very much along the typical general market/multicultural market divide. The company had the traditional black, Hispanic, and Asian human resources resource groups and bucketed its customer base the same way.

But this old system is breaking down. Verizon's total address-able market is heading toward 50 percent New Majority. Mean-while, as of this writing, only one-quarter of the company's subscribers fall into that demographic. That's a problem. Its gross adds—a telecom measure of new customers—among millennial Hispanics and blacks have slipped dramatically over the past two years, even as the demographic picture went the opposite direction. A basic strengths, weaknesses, opportunities, and threats analysis shows that Verizon still has the best product around, but it is hampered by ossified plans and a fragmented structure. The opportunity is clear—New Majority customers aren't just the fastest-growing segment; they spend more per capita, too. Of course, the competitors realize this, too, and they're already focused on this market.

What's a brand to do?

In Verizon's case, the answer is clear. It must restructure its entire enterprise. With Javier's arrival, Verizon is solidly at level 2 in its Total Market readiness. A year from now, it may be a Total Market master.

Verizon has the plan, which we'll discuss in the next chapter. It has the talent. But does it have the will?

And do you? Once your organization knows where it sits in its evolution to the Total Market Enterprise, it is time to start making the organizational changes needed to advance it along. They will be painful and will challenge entrenched groups and old ways of doing things. They'll force you to discuss race within the work-place and marketing in ways you may not yet be comfortable with, and they'll lay your prejudice out in front of you—no matter your race.

In the next chapter, we'll lay out my system for restructuring organizations large and small to prepare for the Total Market. And I'll share Verizon's plans for transformation.

Chapter 7

Step Two: Structuring Your Organization

Javier Farfan, whom you met in the last chapter, exudes casualness—from his beat-up Chuck Taylors to his slightly tousled hair. When he talks about his life, it sounds like he's thinking about it all for the first time, reminiscing in wide-eyed wonder at the fortuitous chain of events that landed him at Verizon with a mandate to turn the place into a New Majority monster.

Don't buy the nonchalance.

Javier is way too smart to make a move without a clear plan—a suspicion he confirms when he mentions that his office décor isn't just soothing to his taste. It's there to send a clear message. His Columbia Business School diploma sits next to an early copy of the hip-hop magazine he cofounded. Jay Z's on the cover—that is, the old Jay Z, the Brooklyn guy who was just being discovered. Jay Z's eyes stare ahead, as if he's watching the Spanish-language hip-hop playing on Javier's TV.

Javier's office is a performance, as is he to an extent—and a damn good one at that. The office projects Javier's cross-cultural credentials, only along two separate axes. Javier spans Hispanic, black, and Asian culture; at the same time, his reach extends from the streets to the pinnacle of the Ivy League and from the hit-driven music business to the rigidly analyzed world of Accenture consulting. Javier's bona fides as a change agent are written into his biography.

Javier works in marketing, and he's technically responsible for the multicultural segment. But that's not what he sees as being his job—and his boss, Diego Scotti, agrees. Both men want to use their remits to transform Verizon's business into a leader for the next generation, not just this one. And that means transforming the whole enterprise, not just the marketing department.

What Does a Total Market Enterprise Organization Look Like?

Before we can get into what a Total Market Enterprise is, we need to understand the other, older ways of marketing. That classic marketing organization model is shown in Figure 7.1.

This is how many large companies are still structured when it comes to marketing. There are some substantial advantages to this way of doing business. The agency is a single-point contact as a center of marketing excellence, and the brands themselves determine their own priorities. Consumer research is cost-effective because of economies of scale.

The marketing department in this scenario is just that: marketing and nothing else. The chief marketing officer in this scenario sometimes reports to the chief executive officer but often does

MODEL 1				PROS
CHIEF MARKETING OFFICER			CHIEF REVENUE OFFICER	• Brands determine focus and investment priority • Agency partner center of excellence • Research efficiency
VP OF MKT./ BRANDS	VP RESEARCH	VP OF ADV.	VICE PRESIDENT CUST. MKT.	**CONS**
DIR. OF MKT./ BRANDS	DIR. RESEARCH	DIR. OF ADV.	DIRECTOR CUST. MKT.	• No owner of growth • Deprioritized to focus on category or financial priority
MGR. MKT./ BRANDS	MGR. RESEARCH	MGR. OF ADV.	KEY ACCOUNT MANAGER	• Little to no shared knowledge base

FIGURE 7.1   The classic marketing organization model

not. Most large enterprises see brand and marketing as soft departments. They spin off reams of data, but most of it is indirect, measuring impressions, views, reach, share of mind, brand drivers, customer journeys, customer lifetime value, and uncounted other factors. Although this data is important—crucial, even—it seems maddeningly imprecise when compared to things such as cost of goods sold, earnings, or revenue per sale. That's the hard science of business—and that's where, historically, C-suite executives and boards have been most comfortable.

As the consumer's power has increased along with demands for corporate transparency, companies have come to understand that their brand isn't just something to stick on the packaging. It is, in many respects, the single most valuable asset that they have— worth protecting, nurturing, and growing. Businesses aren't stupid, and they're not slow either. Marketing is rapidly becoming one of the most crucial corporate functions there is. The rise of the Total Market will only accelerate this change, because it is after all a fundamental change in the nature of the market itself. Who better than marketers to meet that challenge?

The model shown in Figure 7.2 is becoming increasingly popular.

Now there's a new role in the picture—a marketer who is responsible for the multicultural market. This is the role I used to occupy at Miller Brewing. Now there's a multicultural center of excellence in the enterprise that can counterbalance the ad

MODEL 2				PROS
CHIEF MARKETING OFFICER			CHIEF REVENUE OFFICER	• Multicultural center of excellence • Direct link to agency partner and cascade effect • Integration with priority brand(s)
VP OF MKT./ BRANDS	VP RESEARCH	VP OF ADV.	VP CUST. MKT.	**CONS**
DIR. OF MKT./ BRANDS	DIR. RESEARCH	MULTICULTURAL ADV. DIRECTOR	DIRECTOR CUST. MKT.	• Limited or no scale of resources • Minimum impact to enterprise • Constantly making and remaking the business
MGR. MKT./ BRANDS	MGR. RESEARCH	MGR. OF ADV.	KEY ACCOUNT MANAGER	impact case

FIGURE 7.2 An updated marketing model

agency. That leads to a better understanding of the market. Moreover, the enterprise now has a single person responsible for integration with the multicultural agencies, thus creating efficiencies in how their services are used. Of course, this removes the direct contact from the brands, because they now filter through the multicultural-advertising director, but chances are he or she is far more expert in those markets anyway.

The problem with a structure like this is that it solidifies the idea of multicultural marketing as a *separate segment*— one that receives a small share of the marketing pie, and that is engaged in a constant fight to justify increased investment. When multicultural marketing is siloed like this, it has only limited impact on the organization as a whole. This is a setup to continue with separate but equal style marketing. Unless you've got a change agent like Javier Farfan in your company, this is not a model for growth.

Any organization that wants to take advantage of the massive demographic shifts needs to break the multicultural silo and empower a senior marketer to transform the stance of the entire business into one that's fit for the total addressable market. To do that, I recommend a structure like what you see in Figure 7.3.

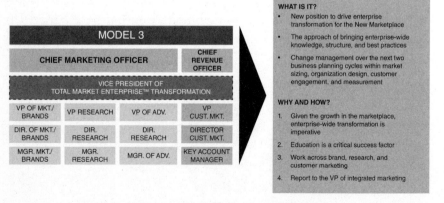

FIGURE **7.3**   The Total Market Enterprise marketing model

You can see how the corporation adds a newly created position in this model—one person responsible for transforming the company into a Total Market Enterprise. This structure has the advantage of spreading Total Market knowledge and best practices across the whole organization. A vice president of Total Market Enterprise transformation knows that growth will come from the New Majority and has no illusions about what his or her job is. This person is there to drive change over two, maybe three, business planning cycles, in the following areas:

- Market sizing
- Organizational design
- Customer engagement
- Measurement

To accomplish that, the director of Total Market Enterprise Transformation will have to work with human resources, brand marketing, consumer marketing, research, and learning and development. At the same time, this person will need to educate the entire C-suite about the Total Market; remake marketing, sales, and operations around servicing this market; incorporate the work of the talent and diversity practices; and keep the leadership of the finance function focused on the gain to come after all the pain is done.

What Is the Total Market Enterprise Execution Road Map?

Transforming to a Total Market Enterprise will take between 12 and 18 months and will require a dedicated sponsor who is focused on the change for that entire time. The details of how the change rolls out will be unique for every organization, but some commonalities always seem to exist. Figure 7.4 is the general road map I use to tell my clients what is in store for them.

Description	Lay the Foundation (6–8 Months)	Systematic Change (6–8 Months)	Institutionalize the Shift (8–12 Months)
People	X	X	X
Process	X	X	X
Systems	X	X	X
Tools	X		X

FIGURE 7.4   Transforming to a Total Market Enterprise

The three main stages of the transformation are listed along the top, and areas for particular focus are shaded. No matter what your organization's Total Market Enterprise level is, you will need to undergo these three stages. Let's look at them in detail.

Lay the Foundation

♦ **People:** Laying the foundation for Total Market transformation may initially seem frustrating. After all, your enterprise wouldn't be embarking on this kind of change without a firm commitment already. However, alignment among decision makers does not guarantee that the organization itself understands what is going on and why it needs to take these steps. Some people don't understand what a Total Market Enterprise is, why it is important, and how this represents a change from multicultural marketing. Others see the numbers and focus in on what appears to be the main chance: Hispanic population growth. Why, they wonder, muck about with all this Total Market crap? Why not just go after the Hispanics and call it a day? So, the aim of laying the foundation is to *build awareness* among key stakeholders, executives, and high-performing teams.

♦ **Process:** Assess the organization's current level. Based on that, you need to lay out your plans and set up educational programs.

♦ **Systems and Tools:** Align success criteria to Total Market measures, and set up a way to measure adoption of Total Market principles.

Drive Systemic Change

♦ **People:** Once the foundation is in place, you can start making greater headway with more people. Your organization now has a coterie of people who understand the New Majority and who can in turn educate their colleagues about the Total Market opportunity. Start up the internal messaging machine; take the Total Market on the road to other teams, disciplines, and customers; set up training programs; and run workshops. The organization is *building the Total Market discipline.*

♦ **Process:** Every big company uses some sort of talent review process. Incorporate Total Market transformation measures into yours. Now is the time to seed market readiness. This is a big change, and you need to make sure your customers and business partners are aware of it. For the change to happen, it needs to be part of the business plans. You should start making tactical market moves with the Total Market in mind. Strategy is your next front. Make sure your annual planning strategy starts from a Total Market point of view. Develop comprehensive systems for analyzing and prioritizing new and emerging businesses. You'll need a streamlined and flexible market and business development that increases your speed to market (without undue risk).

♦ **Systems and Tools:** Build a Total Market learning and development community through technology within the organization. Bring all the existing diversity communities and learning tools into it. Set up a system for informal recognition and incentives for Total Market achievement. Currently this is done through organizational culture and talent feedback systems. However, new tools are in the offing that will integrate these talent and cultural assessments with Total Market Enterprise financial metrics. See Chapter 10 for more on this.

Institutionalize the Shift

♦ **People:** Over this, the longest phase of transformation, your corporation is learning to accept the Total Market shift. Coaching and leadership has to continue unabated, and you must embed the institutional shift deeply in the enterprise. Build career paths that take the Total Market into account, and make sure training gives way to objective setting and metrics. It's no longer time to be learning about the Total Market; it's time to be *acting on it*. Regional and local offices and sales teams have probably only been lightly exposed to the Total Market until now. This is the moment to rework sales enablement around the New Majority and to rework territories and key areas around regional and local Total Market hotspots.

♦ **Process:** The first set of results from Total Market thinking should be coming in. Bake those into the annual business review and make investment decisions accordingly. The annual review and compensation equity systems will need to be reworked so that Total Market penetration is keyed to individual employee incentives. Now that the sales team is prepared for the Total Market, start shifting budget around in accordance with the opportunity. This means that certain regional and local population clusters will start to see more investment dollars from you while your overall marketing budget will start to look more like a reflection of the actual marketplace.

♦ **Systems and Tools:** Some teams will inevitably perform better than others. These are the ones to recognize formally.

You may want to organize them into a Total Market center of excellence, which can be the standard-bearer and consulting expert organization for Total Market transformation in the entire organization. Transform what they've learned into a set of tools to be shared across the organization. Don't ignore thought leadership. Get key executives talking about your transformation externally and make sure you've set up a new Total Market playbook for internal training. Finally, build Total Market into your corporate data dashboard.

Verizon has only just begun its Total Market Enterprise transformation as of this writing, but it made serious progress in its first 60 days. Not only has it assessed itself, but it's also come to grips with the institutional impediments to making change. Armed with that knowledge, it's starting to break some old habits.

Since the launch of its transformation, Verizon has set aside the general market/multicultural divide. It rolled up all of its fragmented categories into one budget built to be allocated by Total Market standards. Gone is the almost-atomized multicultural budget spread out across 30 microtargeted activities. With that kind of fragmentation, nothing could ever have enough oomph behind it to make a dent. Now the company looks at its full budget in terms of cultural engagement, and it's coming to see that further transformation is needed. The budget is still much too heavily weighted toward old demographic trends, but now that conversation can be held based on the total budget instead of based on a percentage increase over the prior year. That might seem like a small matter, but if you've ever sat through a corporate budget meeting, you know that a perception shift like that can make all the difference in the world.

Verizon has also completed an analysis of where its growth will come from. It's all in the New Majority segments—with an emphasis on several crucial regional and local clusters. It's

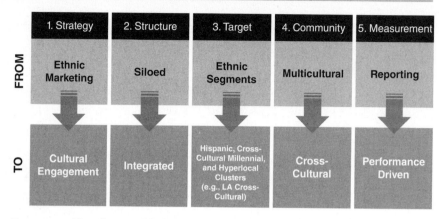

FIGURE **7.5** The changes Verizon needs to make

going after those populations while defending its lead everywhere else.

The company has also embarked on its internal change. Under Javier's leadership, it's transforming the multicultural-marketing group from an ethnically segmented organization to one that builds cultural engagement among millennials and the New Majority. The rest of the enterprise will soon follow along—because the path to follow will have already been blazed.

Verizon is at the start, but it's moving fast. Figure 7.5 shows how the company sees the changes it has to make—and it knows it needs to make them, as Verizon itself puts it, "at the speed of culture."

As I said before, every enterprise must find its own way to make this transformation. Figure 7.5 lays out Verizon's. Yours may look different, but as you can see, this example hits on every aspect of being a Total Market Enterprise.

No matter what your organization ends up looking like, it is going to have to understand its new customers very well. Firms spend huge sums of money every year on research tools, customer segmentations, and needs-and-wants analysis. So, they are to be excused if they think they've got this part nailed. But new markets need new research. The old data purports to be representative, but the truth is that it is based on a skewed population sample. It's time for a revolution in consumer research, as you'll learn in the next chapter.

Chapter **8**

Step Three: Rethinking Your Consumers and Customers

M arket research is big business. $10 billion big. That's a lot of money spent figuring out how consumers feel and behave. These days, the majority of that money goes toward quantitative research.

"Quantitative research" has such a rich and authoritative sound. It's the kind of thing you could trot out during dinner party conversation to hush the room. Who's going to argue with quantitative research?

I am.

I think quantitative research is great. I depend on it for understanding all aspects of the Total Market. My problem is not with the method. It's with the way populations are sampled. As a result of that, month after month, year after year, brands make the decision to invest in audience segments that are not growing. It sounds dramatic, but that's the result of the way consumer research is done. Perhaps I should explain.

Do you recall the Association of National Advertisers (ANA) from earlier in the book? They were the folks who promulgated that gobbledygook definition of the Total Market I took a swipe at before. Well, the ANA isn't the only advertising trade association. The other big one is the American Association of Advertising Agencies, commonly known as the 4A's. Those two organizations pooled their resources to found the Advertising Research Foundation (ARF) way back in 1936. The ARF is a nonprofit industry association that exists to improve the effectiveness of advertising, marketing, and research. It supplies research, runs conferences, and publishes highly respected papers and periodicals. It also sets the standards for audience measurement and copy testing—two crucial parts of the marketing research universe. Given the age of the ARF, it should come as no surprise that these standards were set in the 1950s. Despite modification over the years, the ARF standards, which drive the work of all the research firms, are still very in thrall to the general market/multicultural market divide. The money, moreover, is in general-market research, thus perpetuating the problem. General-market agencies are the ones with the funds to pay for research, and, as a result, the highest-quality research focuses on an out-of-date demographic sample. Should research firms decide to do Total Market research, they'll find another problem—talent. The lack of diversity in general-market advertising is also found in general-market research firms. And that makes it hard to generate meaningful cross-cultural insights. How can a firm with only one dominant culture ever hope to portray the cross-cultural experience? Even if it were able to develop the insights and data, it has a credibility problem when it comes to delivering the information.

Multicultural agencies use research. So, it must come from somewhere, right? Yes, there are an increasing number of multicultural data points available to agencies. Many (if not all) market researchers are tracking this now, but they've been doing so only since around the turn of the century. The tradition of using agency research for multicultural marketing is, therefore, still emerging. Instead, multicultural marketers turned to ad hoc, one-off research projects, which were inconsistent in quality and not suitable for cross-reference or longitudinal analysis.

It's worth celebrating the fact that large subscription-based agencies are including appropriate multicultural sampling in their work. But because they are still segregating it into two distinct market verticals, I believe it's a doomed project. Before too long, both sets of data will drift further and further from the reality of daily life in a cross-cultural world. Until the research agencies collapse the categories and start to look at the Total Market, the research findings agencies and marketers use will continue to be inaccurate.

We're starting to see some change, however, and research organizations, such the ARF, are beginning to understand the opportunity research tools for the total addressable market present.

Total Addressable Market

This is a concept we've talked about a bit before, but I think it's worth looking more deeply. Take a look at Figure 8.1.

The total addressable market (or TAM) describes the size of the *revenue opportunity* available for a product or service. For

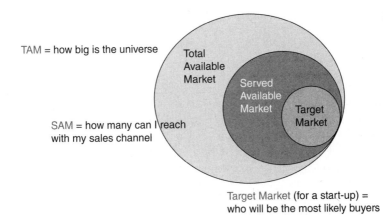

TAM = how big is the universe

Total Available Market

Served Available Market

Target Market

SAM = how many can I reach with my sales channel

Target Market (for a start-up) = who will be the most likely buyers

Fɪɢᴜʀᴇ **8.1** Total Available Market, Served Available Market, and Target Market

Source: https://en.wikipedia.org/wiki/Total_addressable_market

that reason, it's also referred to as the total available market. The TAM helps companies prioritize business opportunities by giving enterprises a way of understanding the overall potential of any given market segment. Companies rely on the TAM to size the market, but they don't expect that giant number to flow down to their balance sheets. TAM is the first step in assessing the population a company can reach. The served available market (or SAM) is the size of the population an enterprise can reach via its channels. SAM is a fraction—sometimes huge and sometimes tiny—of the TAM. The smallest number of all is the target market. These are the folks who are the most likely buyers. No company has the marketing resources to market to the entirety of its SAM, much less the TAM. So, it looks more deeply at the demographic and psychographic characteristics of its likely customers and markets to others in the SAM who fit those criteria.

Effective targeted marketing is the essence of efficient spending for a company. It's what puts your brand in front of the right people, at the right time, and via the right channels. But as you can see now, the composition of what you think your target market is can be off base. When a company has the wrong idea about the TAM, that error is repeated in the SAM and then again in the target market. Companies could be—hell, they are—marketing to a small fraction of the people who may be interested in their goods and services.

Research standards from more than a half century ago are ill equipped to reflect the demographic realities today, and as a result the quantitative studies that companies—from giant to just starting out—rely on don't sample the New Majority appropriately. As a result, huge marketing decisions are made based on an incorrect TAM, an incorrect SAM, and an incorrect target market.

That's why the first step in any transformation to being a Total Market Enterprise has to contain a reevaluation of a company's TAM.

The Brand Cross-Cultural Index

I'd like to highlight one new research source—the Brand Cross-Cultural Index—that paves the way for other large research agencies to decode the Total Market. The Brand Cross-Cultural Index is the product of collaboration between Ogilvy & Mather and Millward Brown, and it represents one of the initial forays into market research built from the ground up with the Total Market in mind.

Rather than starting from scratch with new data, the Brand Cross-Cultural Index is based on Millward Brown's BrandZ brand equity database. (We chose BrandZ because of its market-leading reputation and size.) Using that data, we created two major metrics for marketers:

♦ A Brand Cross-Cultural Index (BCCI) Ranking that identifies which brands do the best job nurturing a meaningful connection with consumers across all racial or ethnic segments of the population—whites included. The analysis also determines a brand's Multicultural Opportunity (MCO), which helps identify which ethnic segments drive the BCCI up or down.

♦ Brand Power, a cross-cultural equity analysis that allows brand owners to pinpoint growth opportunities and under-stand the revenue potential of increasing marketing spend for particular groups.

We calculated the BCCI Ranking and the MCO using some-thing called the Meaningfully Different framework that Millward Brown uses in its measures of brand equity. This framework score measures the extent to which brands build an emotional connection with consumers and are seen to deliver against functional needs. It shows how, as we say in the BCCI, "impres-sions of brands—as meaningful, different and salient—influence purchase behavior. Depending on how meaningful, different and salient these brand impressions are, consumers are going to be more or less predisposed to choose a brand over others and pay more for it." Our underlying assumption was that brands that are more cross-cultural are better able to establish a meaningful connection with consumers across ethnicities whereas less cross-cultural brands appeal to just a few of them.

We found that some brands—Toyota, Coca-Cola, and Hennessy Cognac—were maximizing the multicultural opportunity while others were falling behind.

Now, here's where things get interesting. We found that leading among blacks, Hispanics, and Asians didn't necessarily mean that a brand was the strongest across the Total Market. Some brands, such as Subway, are so strong among whites that their relative underperformance in multicultural segments doesn't hurt them.

Or I should say, it doesn't hurt them *yet*. Brands need to understand where they rank among their peers in multicultural segments, and they need to understand what the multicultural opportunity looks like for them.

Figure 8.2 shows what the rankings for three major categories look like.

Things change a little bit if we add another factor in—Brand Power. Brand Power predicts how much of a brand's total volume in the marketplace is because of perception alone. No in-store marketing, coupons, and so on. Just what folks think about the brand. This data, when combined with the BCCI and MCO scores, allows brands to calculate exactly how much revenue they can gain by increasing various connection factors among individual ethnic groups. Consider the quick-service restaurant Sonic. Sonic has a total Brand Power rating of 4.2 percent. That's smack in the middle of the pack for the category. However, if Sonic were to increase its connection to ethnic

	QSR				Beer				Banking		
Rk	Brand	BCCI	MCO	Rk	Brand	BCCI	MCO	Rk	Brand	BCCI	MCO
1	Subway	139	90	1	Heineken	120	126	1	Chase	123	108
2	McDonald's	130	103	2	Corona	118	115	2	Wells Fargo	115	97
3	Panera	125	94	3	Bud Light	116	96	3	Bank of America	115	126
4	Chipotle	122	126	4	Coors Light	115	90	4	US Bank	100	94
5	Chick Fil-A	119	107	5	Yuengling	114	102	5	Ally Bank	99	97
6	Wendy's	109	91	6	Samuel Adams	108	67	6	BB&T	98	105
7	Burger King	106	92	7	Blue Moon	107	99	7	Capital One	96	109
8	Taco Bell	101	96	8	Budweiser	105	110	8	PNC Bank	96	73
9	KFC	99	98	9	Stella Artois	102	113	9	TD Bank	95	93
10	Pizza Hut	96	110	10	Dos Equis	101	103	10	Regions	94	77
11	Popeyes	94	120	11	Guinness	99	98	11	Key Bank	94	95
12	Starbucks	93	108	12	Miller Lite	95	83	12	M&T Bank	91	69
13	Dairy Queen	88	90	13	Modelo	93	106	13	Citibank	89	108
14	Arby's	88	85	14	Michelob	91	96	14	Sun Trust	88	100
15	Jack in the Box	86	117	15	MGD	90	111	15	Fifth Third	87	90
16	Sonic	86	93	16	Miller High Life	87	109	16	HSBC	86	104
17	Papa John's	85	105	17	Keystone Light	83	98	17	Citizens Bank	84	93
18	Dunkin's Donuts	83	93	18	Busch	81	100				
19	Domino's Pizza	82	104	19	Natural Light	79	95				
20	Carl's Jr.	82	98	20	Pabst Blue Ribbon	78	90				
21	Hardee's	80	97								

Figure 8.2 BCCI and MCO rankings across three categories

Note: QSR stands for quick-service restaurants.

consumers in just a couple of areas—meaning and salience—it could see revenue growth of up to *$248 million*. That's a pretty strong argument for rebalancing marketing spending!

The Winning Brands

I've shown you the cross-cultural index for three categories. We've actually done it for 13 separate categories by now. Let's look at how this all works in more depth.

As we've said, brands with the highest BCCI scores have the most meaningful relationship with consumers. Figure 8.3 shows the best-performing brands and their BCCI scores.

Verizon, as you can see, connects well with consumers. But given what you already know, you won't be surprised to find it absent from the next chart (Figure 8.4). This next set of brands is the ranking of those with the highest MCO scores. These are the brands that generate the most rapport among multicultural consumers.

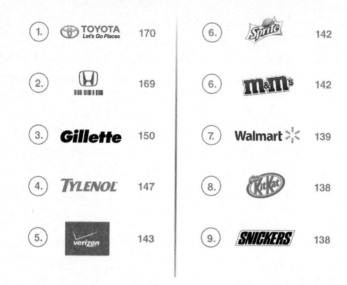

FIGURE 8.3   The top ten brands by BCCI

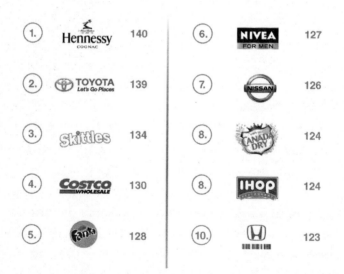

FIGURE 8.4   The top ten brands by MCO

RK	BRAND	BCCI	MCO
1	Verizon	143	78
2	C Spire Wireless	115	81
3	AT&T	109	92
4	Straight Talk Wireless	102	114
5	TracFone	100	106
6	T-Mobile	100	105
7	CenturyLink	98	114
8	MetroPCS	97	102
9	Sprint	94	106
10	Virgin Mobile	92	103
11	Cricket Wireless	92	104
12	US Cellular	90	103
13	Boost Mobile	89	113
14	Vonage	73	112

FIGURE **8.5** Communications sector rankings

Only two brands, Toyota and Honda, appear on both lists. They are the only brands successfully pursuing a Total Market strategy right now.

Verizon has disappeared, and you can see why when you look at the ranking of companies in the communications category in Figure 8.5.

Several brands are overindexing among New Majority consumers, but none of them is hitting it out of the park. Given the importance of mobile communications in New Majority communities, this is a major missed opportunity. That's why Verizon is working hard to raise its MCO score from 79. If it can translate its size and the consumer connection it has with whites into a strong New Majority position, it will be indomitable.

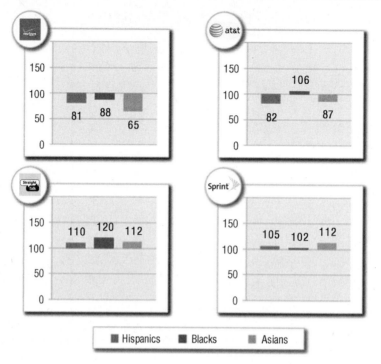

FIGURE 8.6 The relative position of major telecom providers across New Majority segments

As you can see in Figure 8.6, it has its work cut out for it. Shown are the MCO rankings for the three key New Majority ethnic groups for Verizon, AT&T, Straight Talk, and Sprint. Although AT&T is making some progress with black consumers, it's got a ways to go with Hispanics and Asians. Verizon, on the other hand, is getting killed in every New Majority category. This figure paints a very clear picture of the future. If these rankings don't change, then demographic changes will result in large competitors, such as Sprint and T-Mobile, taking over leadership in the communications sector while start-ups, such as Straight Talk, may move from being niche players to major factors.

Grocery is another interesting category. Figure 8.7 shows the rankings for the major players.

RK	BRAND	BCCI	MCO
1	Walmart	139	108
2	Super Target	130	113
3	Publix	113	88
4	Costco	113	130
5	H-E-B	110	101
6	Kroger	108	85
7	Trader Joe's	100	90
8	Aldi	98	100
9	Sam's Club	95	104
10	Stop & Shop	92	110
11	Whole Foods	91	96
12	Safeway	89	100
13	Albertson's	88	97
14	Hy-Vee	86	68
15	Meijer	86	82
16	Giant Food	86	91
17	Harris Teeter	83	90
18	Ingles	83	107
19	Save-A-Lot	79	98
20	Food Lion	75	85
21	Winn-Dixie	72	83
22	Giant Eagle	72	84
23	Fred Meyer	70	80

FIGURE **8.7** Grocery sector rankings

This chart tells a different sort of story. Walmart and Costco have strong BCCI and MCO rankings. Walmart depends a little more on the white audience whereas Costco, with a higher MCO than BCCI, relies on multicultural strength to a greater degree. Still, both brands are clearly strong with both sets of consumers. Great. Game on, right? Well, this is where cross-cultural understanding comes in. With its strong focus on price, Walmart has made great inroads among blacks and been less successful with Hispanics and Asians (see Figure 8.8).

Costco, on the other hand, has connected with all ethnic groups. Despite its smaller size, Costco is better positioned for the future (see Figure 8.9).

Kroger, however, is in trouble. It may be one of the dominant and best-loved grocery chains in the country now, but look how poorly it connects to Asians, blacks, and especially Hispanics (see

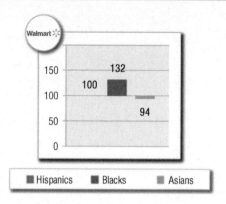

FIGURE 8.8 Performance across New Majority segments for Walmart

Figure 8.10). If its numbers continue like this, Kroger will soon become irrelevant.

I'm particularly fascinated by the changes in the men's care category. This used to be what we call a "low-interest" category. It was sort of the toilet paper of beauty brands. (Do you really think about your toilet paper choice? Or do you just stumble down the aisle and pick out whichever "soft and strong" brand you bought last time, unless something else is on sale?) Men tend to be creatures of habit when it comes to grooming. My coauthor has never even *tried* a razor that wasn't made by Gillette. Things started to change recently, though. Men became much more interested in premium personal grooming. Many factors have gone into this

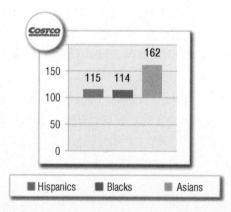

FIGURE 8.9 Performance across New Majority segments for Costco

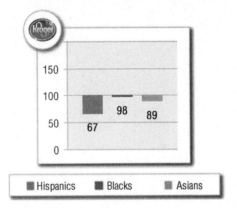

Figure 8.10 Performance across New Majority segments for Kroger

change, but I believe the most significant one is the influence of lesbian, gay, bisexual, and transgender (LGBT) culture on the mainstream. It's one of the prime effects of cross-culturalism and one of the clearest examples of how cultural exchange is leading to the creation of a new type of mass culture. Not being stupid, brands rushed in. Old Spice came back with a vengeance. Nivea (I've always wondered if that name came from spelling—phoneti- cally—the word *heaven* backward) started a men's line, and so did Dove. These new premium men's grooming lines started posting impressive growth, often outstripping the growth rates of their parent brands. Old Spice also grew fast, despite being a venerable name. It reinvented itself as hip, hilarious, and ironic. If Dove and Nivea were the guys you wanted to be your wingmen, Old Spice was the guy you wanted to be. Old Spice's famous commercials, featuring Isaiah Mustafa, played into that. Because no sane guy would ever turn down the chance to look like the now-famous actor, the ads made that their central joke. The results were viral fame and a reinvigorated brand.

I should mention here, in case you don't remember from Chapter 3, that Isaiah Mustafa is black. So, it may surprise you to learn that despite its reemergence into relevance and its famous black brand icon, Old Spice has one of the lowest MCOs in the category (see Figure 8.11).

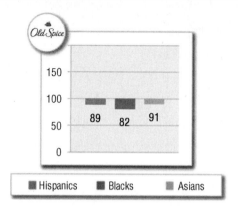

FIGURE **8.11**   Performance across New Majority segments for Old Spice

Contrast that with the scores from Dove and Nivea (Figure 8.12).

So, what gives? I think the answer can be found in the age of the brands. Old Spice is a legacy product that's been refreshed whereas Dove Men+Care and Nivea for Men are newer lines built from scratch with the demographic realities of today in mind. You can see this in every aspect of these businesses, from distribution to product mix to advertising. Old Spice, by contrast, is relying on a black face in its ads to show off its multicultural cred. That doesn't cut it, especially because it's trading on the old, racist trope of the hypervirile black man.

FIGURE **8.12**   Performance across New Majority segments for Dove and Nivea

RK	BRAND	BCCI	MCO
1	Bacardi	127	110
2	Grey Goose	127	105
3	Smirnoff	123	109
4	Absolut	120	107
5	Patrón	119	103
6	Baileys	115	83
7	Jose Cuervo	104	95
8	Jack Daniel's	98	80
9	Crown Royal	98	98
10	Captain Morgan	97	90
11	Hennessy	93	140
12	Svedka	92	104
13	Johnnie Walker	89	105
14	Jameson	82	91
15	Jim Beam	80	78
16	Seagram's Gin	74	105
17	Tanqueray	72	84
18	Jägermeister	48	116

FIGURE **8.13**   Spirits sector rankings

The spirits category teaches us a different lesson (see Figure 8.13).

As you know, alcohol consumption is heavily tied in with identity and culture. When I was growing up, for example, blacks didn't drink much beer because bar culture wasn't a part of our lives. Young blacks went out to clubs, not bars. And at clubs, you get mixed drinks. At that time, the spirit of choice was some form of brown liquor. Around the turn of the century, beer brands started to focus on blacks, trying to build in a culture of beer drinking. They made some, but not much, impact. The real noise in beer was in the Hispanic marketplace. The spirit brands, by contrast, found a motivated, growing market ready to embrace something new. They borrowed the cultural currency of key celebrities to introduce new spirits into the community. This was an easier sell because of the existing club culture, and it worked brilliantly. Celebrity

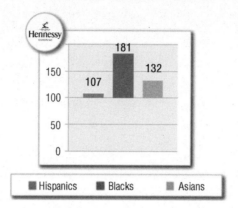

Figure 8.14 Performance across New Majority segments for Hennessy

combined with ongoing brand investment (or, as we'll discuss in the next chapter, Cultural Currency plus Cultural Community) to establish a new go-to spirit for blacks. The biggest winner was Hennessy Cognac, although Smirnoff Vodka and Bacardi Rum weren't far behind (see Figure 8.14).

The keys here were embracing black artists, building credibility with rap music, and supporting cultural and charity events. In addition, the brand deployed impressive on-the-ground resources to get its liquors promoted to the bartenders in the clubs. One part credibility mixed with one part commitment, one part celebrity, and one part presence makes for a tasty drink, at least as far as Hennessy Cognac's chief financial officer is concerned.

I mentioned earlier that Toyota appears to be the champion Total Market Enterprise right now (see Figure 8.15).

Why is it—and to a lesser extent, Honda—dominant in both the BCCI and MCO index? I think it is because they have tapped into core human benefits—benefits that transcend ethnicity—which they then communicate in a culturally relevant way. The company is associated with trust and quality, and everyone wants that. Toyota activates that equity by capitalizing on demographic

RK	BRAND	BCCI	MCO
1	Toyota	170	139
2	Honda	169	123
3	Ford	124	87
4	Chevrolet	120	104
5	Nissan	120	126
6	Hyundai	90	95
7	GMC	82	75
8	Jeep	81	80
9	Mazda	79	90
10	Dodge	79	87
11	VW (Volkswagen)	79	107
12	Subaru	78	81
13	Chrysler	76	93
14	Buick	76	85
15	Kia	75	95

Figure 8.15   Automobile sector rankings

shifts. It no longer splits out its multicultural efforts and, instead, reaches out to the combined New Majority. As a result, Toyota sells more cars to blacks, Hispanics, and Asians than any other automobile company sells (see Figure 8.16).

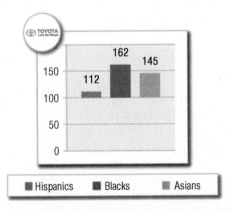

Figure 8.16   Performance across New Majority segments for Toyota

Just a First Step

I've dwelt on the BCCI because I know it best. I helped develop it and have coauthored each of the two reports issued on it. However, using BCCI is only one way of providing high-quality Total Market insight to brands. Every research organization should be developing its own offering based on its own special sauce. Armed with tools like these, a brand can assess exactly what the future looks like for it and get enough data to make an educated decision about how to move into a New Majority world. Is a comprehensive Total Market solution, like Toyota's the right choice? How about a deep dive into a single segment, like Hennessy Cognac? Or maybe it's a reboot to face nimbler, more culturally relevant competitors, as Verizon is doing. Regardless of the direction your brand takes, the right customer experience is going to be at the heart of it. As we'll see in the next chapter, there are several strategies a brand can use to be a trusted part of the New Majority's world. None of these strategies is cheap or easy. Authenticity cannot be faked, particularly for the savvy millennial consumer.

Chapter 9

Step Four: Designing the Right Customer Experience

This book began with marketing, just as my career did. And it is to marketing that we need to return now. We discussed audits, structures, and market assessment, and now we circle back to the customer. As you saw in the last chapter, Toyota rules when it comes to Total Market success. Honda does a damn good job, too. Those two companies account for four of the top 10 new cars sold in the U.S. Hispanic market. How have those two companies achieved such brand equity in the Total Market?

There is no one factor. It's a combination of reputation, product, quality, price, location, and customer experience. We'll deal with that last factor here because it affects all f the others and because it's the one most sensitive to Total Market thinking. (I should mention that location is a Total Market factor as well, but the solution is laughably simple: Make sure your product is available where New Majority customers live and shop. Got that? Good.)

Over the last 10 years, technology, mobile, and social media tools have made it easier than ever to connect to consumers on a one-to-one basis. Books—hell, libraries—have been written about this, and I'll not add to the deluge. But if you don't have a good grasp of customer relationship management (CRM) and digital engagement, spend a little time reading up.

The key thing to understand for our purposes here is that brands and business did not progress at the same speed that New Majority consumers did.

Being Up Front about the Upfronts

Media is a case in point. As anyone who watches TV will know, the past two years have been a boom time for diverse casting agents. Major shows with black, Hispanic, or Asian leading characters have debuted and soared in the ratings. Despite the trail blazed by Shonda Rhimes, many in television pronounced these shows "surprise" successes. I'm shaking my head. How can an industry that makes its way in the world by giving people what they want to see miss the glaring demographic changes going on right now? Of course people want to see people who look like them, who have similar lives to them, who share cultural experiences with them, hell, who just plain *resemble* them on TV. Storytelling works a lot better (and holds more emotional valence) when the audience identifies with the leading roles. The success of *Blackish*, *Fresh off the Boat*, *Jane the Virgin*, and *Empire* should have been predicted, and it would have been had the television industry completed enough internal change that its creative leadership saw diversity as a competitive advantage.

Still, the sheer number of nonwhite faces on TV is a good thing. As Tao Jones wrote in the *Wall Street Journal*'s *Speakeasy* blog, "Of the 34 new scripted shows picked up for 2015, two-thirds feature nonwhite leads or co-leads, up from about half in 2014."[1] That's a sign that TV is starting to act with some sense. The younger generations—the ones TV advertisers crave—are more diverse than older generations, and the bulk of national population growth is found in those same New Majority sectors. So, it's logical to find TV finally overrepresenting the New Majority. If only it weren't so frustrating . . .

Yes, frustrating. Despite the plethora of diverse programming, the money is still going to shows with, ahem, traditional casts. More than three-quarters of primetime ad space is sold in one huge ad sales orgy called upfronts. The new shows—the ones that are killing it in ratings—are the cheapest media around. As Jones wrote about the 2014–2015 upfronts, "Of the 20 cheapest shows on TV—those with the lowest spot cost relative to the eyeballs they ultimately delivered—six of them were new shows with ethnic leads, with mega-hit 'Empire' at the bottom and 'Fresh Off the Boat' following close after. Meanwhile, 2014–15's 20 most expensive shows included seven new shows with white protagonists." That's awesome for brands eager to reach the New Majority, but it's terrible for people eager to see more shows with diverse talent in front of and behind the camera. Great shows have emerged despite these obstacles, and they'll find an audience in part because of pent-up demand. But ongoing, high-quality New Majority programming depends on the dollars flowing toward the casts, crews, and producers with whom the audience can identify. Consumers are craving those experiences.

Cross-Cultural Experiences

The Total Market consumer is the midst of an engagement lag. She wants omnichannel connection to products and services, and she's not getting it. She expects brands to reflect her lived experience, and she's not getting that either. Let's explore a little deeper and learn how to build the most effective customer engagement opportunities. As we discussed earlier, the bifurcated nature of marketing and communications created deep ethnic insights while creating a separate but equal system of marketing. We understood individual populations very well, but we didn't have equally strong tools to measure business and consumer insight across populations. We didn't excel at using

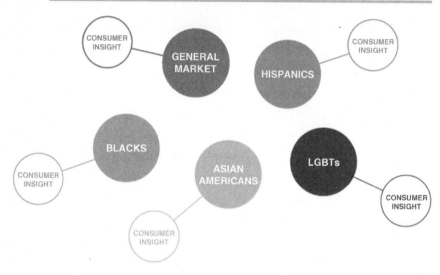

FIGURE 9.1   The General Market and Multicultural Market advertising world

those cultural insights to bear on the brand positioning and communications platform. We underinvested in fast-growing populations and preserved the fiction that general-market culture was still dominant and unchanged. That left us with multiple disconnected platforms and creative strategies. Our world looked like the illustration in Figure 9.1.

Silos work well for niche markets. They're a disaster for large, dynamic marketplaces. Not only is that approach inefficient, but it also ignores all the culture and insight that emerges at the electric boundaries between cultures. To put it simply, that approach assumes that black people have nothing to do with white people, that Hispanics don't interact with Asians, and so on.

That's patently ridiculous, of course. Just think about all the cultural mixing in your life. Think about the wheels on your car. If you bought a car in the last 10 years or so, there's a good chance that the wheel-to-tire ratio is a lot different than it was before. There are solid engineering reasons for that shift. Shorter, stiffer sidewalls improve some handling characteristics. However, the increase in what's called "unsprung weight" can screw up road

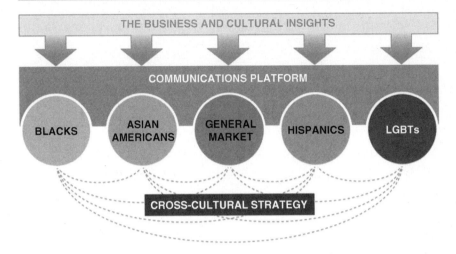

F<small>IGURE</small> **9.2** The cross-cultural model

feel and fuel economy. So, where did this come from? Multi-cultural influences, of course.

There are uncounted other examples of invisible cultural influence in every walk of life. Our culture is already a chaotic flow of information from one group to another, so our customer experience design must reflect that. We need to look at the way we create it anew—we need to look at it like the model shown in Figure 9.2.

This model encourages a brand to create its customer experiences in a new way, but brands and their agency partners struggle to land within the right strategic experience platform. Inspired by David A. Aaker's book published in 1991, *Managing Brand Equity*, I've put together what I believe to be the future of building customer experiences, customer relationships, and, therefore, brand equity, in the New Majority era.

The Five Strategic Territories

When I first started looking into this topic, I interviewed brand, agency, and enterprise stakeholders in both the current general-

market and multicultural spaces. I found my research complicated by the shifting boundaries between the general and multicultural markets. People struggled to pinpoint a transition point
between efforts to serve the various audiences. I viewed that
single unexpected finding as the most important validation yet of
my thesis.

After analyzing the ways in which more than 100 brands were
marketed to Hispanic, Black, Asian American, and lesbian, gay,
bisexual, and transgender (LGBT) audiences separately, I identified certain patterns, which were eventually refined into five key
strategies:

Cultural Community

Cultural Currency

Cultural Authenticity

Cultural Confluence

The Cultural Loop

This is not a change framework as I laid out before. These five
territories are broad categories of marketing ideas and techniques, and they represent a gross oversimplification. I get
that. Marketing is so varied, creative, and evanescent that any
attempt at categorization is going to commit all kinds of intellec-
tual crimes. Still, learning how to market in a Total Market world
needs some sort of structured way of looking at how brands
increase relevancy and equity measures over time. This is my
framework. As you become more adept at marketing in this
manner, yours may stray from mine, and I think that's great.
Today's marketing landscape is morphing rapidly, and brands are
learning to engage through new and emerging channels. We're all
still working out how to build broad-based cross-cultural

strategies that can reach consumers in every channel and at every point along the customer journey.

Figure 9.3 provides an at-a-glance overview of the five strategic territories, what they require of the brand, and how they supply value to the customer and enterprise. Next, we'll go through each strategic territory in more detail.

Strategic Territory 1: Cultural Community

Definition: Participating in long-standing community-based cultural events and programs

People often strongly identify with community-based events that celebrate a shared identity and carry cultural value down from generation to generation. Take, for example, Calle Ocho, a street party staged by Miami's sizable Cuban American population, or the ESSENCE Music Festival, held annually in New Orleans and widely attended by blacks. New York's Columbus Day Parade is an another example, as are all the events that take place around the country on St. Patrick's Day.

These "for the community, by the community" events have traditionally served to strengthen the fabric of cultural communities, bringing extended families and friends together around a common celebration to reinforce identity. For some brands, this is a means of reinforcing their long-standing support for the community. For others, it's an opportunity to introduce the brand to a new set of consumers. The barriers to entry are low, and this can be a low-risk way of opening the door to the longer process of embedding the brand in community culture.

Caters well to: Brands with low cultural relevancy and low cultural equity.

Risk/reward: This strategy produces reward in proportion to the investment. If a brand does nothing more than sponsor the event, it runs the risk of low initial payoff. Buying sponsorship

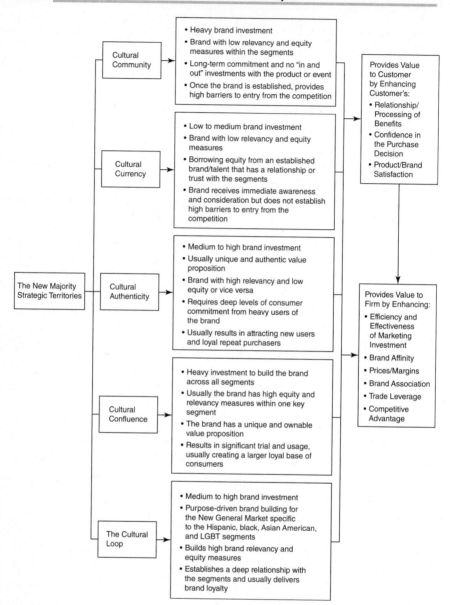

Figure 9.3 The Cross-Cultural Strategic Territory Framework for Building Brand Relevancy and Equity

rights will not likely translate into deep affinity for the brand, at least in the short term.

The benefits come when brands invest time and resources. Done right, the Cultural Community approach requires a long-term commitment; it's the equivalent of the residents of a tight-knit ethnic segment inviting the brands into their homes and offering them the chance to prove they want a relationship. When brands invest in Cultural Community over time, they can enjoy substantial rewards. Demonstrating a commitment to a community's shared culture signals that the brand cares and is here to stay. The community's younger members grow up with the brand and see it as an ally—a friendly entity that's investing in them personally. Long-term brand loyalty often emerges as older generations endorse the products and services they introduce to their progeny.

Calle Ocho   Calle Ocho started in 1978 as a way to showcase Cuban culture in Miami. Today more than 1 million people come from all over the world to attend this street party, which is covered by the press and major networks and sponsored by many top brands. Calle Ocho is renowned for its music, with top Hispanic acts performing during the weekend festival. The list of sponsors mixes Spanish-language media with international brands. One notable sponsor is AT&T. The nation's second-largest wireless provider has access to the same sort of data that Verizon does. It knows the same demographic stories. It also knows that Hispanics don't just represent a demographic growth story. They also represent a better-use case. According to the Pew Research Center's Internet Project, 60 percent of Hispanic mobile Internet users go online mostly via mobile phone. That's dramatically higher than blacks, who come in at 43 percent, or whites, who are even lower at 27 percent. Unfortunately, AT&T has an even lower MCO score than Verizon (although AT&T is doing better with both blacks and Asians). Calle Ocho is one of the many places AT&T is trying to reach Hispanic consumers, and it's a relationship that is likely to continue for quite some time because the brand sees the Hispanic consumer as a key to its future. For example, AT&T's "Between Two Worlds" campaign beautifully articulates the cross-cultural experience from a Hispanic point of view. What AT&T has not done, however, is tie its Hispanic efforts into a larger Total Market framework. Appealing to Hispanics won't alienate the rest of the user base, of course, but its approach won't enable it to migrate the powerful insights that led to "Between Two Worlds" to the rest of the Total Market.

ESSENCE Music Festival   For three days hundreds of thousands gather for concerts and community-based events in New Orleans. According to Michelle Ebanks, president of Essence Communications Inc., "The ESSENCE Music Festival is the ultimate destination for entertainment and inspiration as we gather together to celebrate culture and connect to our community with some of the hottest names in music and entertainment." Now in its eighteenth year, the ESSENCE Music Festival is the nation's definitive African American, live music, and cultural experience, and it has a long-standing sponsorship relationship with Coca-Cola.

Coca-Cola has a long history of sponsorship. From *American Idol* to the Olympic Games, the brand shows up again and again. But Coca-Cola has a problem with the New Majority. The company's Sprite brand is dominant among multicultural consumers because of consistent efforts to reach them via every strategic territory around, but Coke (and especially Diet Coke) has been less consistent. That's a bit of a cruel irony, considering how pioneering Coke was in promoting racial harmony and integration. From its famous Hilltop TV spot to the iconic "Bench" print ad—one of the first mainstream presentations of black and white integration—Coke has always been on the forefront of cross-culturalism. The brand is trying to stage a comeback, however, and given how savvy Coke is with mobile technology and music, it's a good bet that it will succeed.

STRATEGIC TERRITORY 2: CULTURAL CURRENCY

Definition: A partnership with talent or a prominent figure within the community

Sometimes, affinity by association helps. Prominent figures act not only as cultural icons but also as cultural gatekeepers. When a brand builds associations or partnerships with culturally significant talent, it borrows cultural equity to better reach and connect with that segment of consumers.

The usual approach is for a brand to work with a celebrity or entertainment property that shares identity markers with a particular segment and has, therefore, special authority to speak on its behalf. Consumers in the target segment look to culturally significant figures for signals on what to trust (and brands to avoid)—a quasi–litmus test of brand validity.

Caters well to: Brands with low cultural relevancy and low to medium cultural equity.

Risk/reward: As with Cultural Community, the Cultural Currency approach can supply an initial introduction for a brand to a community—a point of entry to establish an audience. Instead of a community-based event, however, the channel for the relationship is through brand association via talent. Additionally, by borrowing cultural equity, brands may reap a particular seal of approval—the equivalent of a reference from a well-trusted source.

But *quick entry* should not be conflated with *low risk*. Partnering through brand association always carries inherent risk. Through association, the brand's equity in that community is tied to the reputation of the talent. Should the talent lose his or her standing in the community, so too might the brand.

Cîroc Vodka   After Diageo partnered with Sean "Diddy" Combs, the brand grew 552 percent from 2007 to 2010, replacing Belvedere as the second-ranked vodka in the ultrapremium category.

Keep in mind that clear liquor wasn't even a factor in the black club culture before the year 2000, but Diddy's entrepreneurial force and reputation for success drove Cîroc to be seen as emblematic of success. And not just any kind of success. Diddy embodied success that stayed true to its cultural roots, and that authenticity rubbed off on the vodka brand.

Samsung Mobile Phone   There are countless engagements with brands and talent, but the Samsung partnership with Jay Z caught my eye. The brand and the Hova teamed up to offer a counterargument to the Apple iPhone. Unlike Apple, Samsung has a strong foothold within the African American and Hispanic communities. However, it missed the cue when it came to launching a sustainable experience platform. It leaned too heavily on the talent partnership and failed to leverage the equity they had within multicultural segments.

STRATEGIC TERRITORY 3: CULTURAL AUTHENTICITY
Definition: Connecting with the New Majority based on insights driven from specific communities outward or vice versa

Most often, brands are practiced at connecting to a general-market audience with which they're familiar, but they struggle with building connection in a cross-cultural way. As opposed to making an introduction (say, through an event sponsorship), the Cultural Authenticity approach is a process of getting to know people. Brands develop authentic relationships through uncovering and nurturing relevant cultural insights.

The best examples come from brands that use an insight most relevant to a particular community. Distilling cultural insights requires serious research, influencing everything from product and service development to communications. Ultimately, the approach calls for a high degree of insight and a dedication to reflecting it in the marketplace.

Caters well to: Brands with high cultural relevancy and low cultural equity, or vice versa.

Risk/reward: Using Cultural Authenticity requires deep levels of understanding and commitment. In other words, it's expensive. The best examples come from brands that create an organic bond with the community.

This requires a heavy investment in research or innovation during the product development cycle, with the particular audience(s) in mind. Sometimes brands get it right from the beginning because of a deep cultural understanding of the Total Market. But in general, Cultural Authenticity is not an easy tactic to execute because it requires a powerful cultural insight delivered holistically through the enterprise organization all the way down to the sales experience. The brands, in effect, become natural extensions of the community. This is one of the tactics Verizon is set to employ. Brands that are successful at executing this strategy often enjoy a long and profitable tenure and erect high barriers to category entry by competitors.

Honey Bunches of Oats   Regardless of fluency, 80 percent of Hispanics want bilingual packaging. The Honey Bunches of Oats "Think Positive" campaign marked the first time the company implemented a bilingual pack promotion. That's a big deal, one that required commitment from the entire organization, from product and packaging all the way through to sales enablement. You can see the results on more than just the packaging. Honey Bunches of Oats' communications are often bilingual—just take a look at all the Spanish ads on its YouTube channel—but more important it is rife with cross-cultural insights, accurately reflecting the way people live now. It gets at a core human truth—that all people want to feel proud of the work they do—and it displays that in a culturally relevant yet universal fashion.

STRATEGIC TERRITORY 4: CULTURAL CONFLUENCE

Definition: Turning a segment's cultural values into attributes relevant to the Total Market

When we reference Cultural Confluence, people sometimes think we're suggesting meshing or watering down the brand, thereby costing the brand its authenticity. This is far from the truth. This cross-cultural approach is more accurately defined as taking a holistic approach to the Total Marketplace.

Caters well to: Brands with medium to high cultural relevancy and medium to high cultural equity.

Risk/reward: Usually brands that are successful at this tactic enjoy strong trial and usage results and get a high degree of repeat usage. This tactic helps brands increase loyalty among a larger base of consumers and establish higher barriers to entry for competitors. We'll see more brands adopting Cultural Confluence strategies as the Total Market becomes more established.

Red Rooster   After a celebrated run as executive chef at Aquavit Restaurant, the Ethiopia-born Marcus Samuelsson opened Red Rooster, a brilliantly reviewed reflection of Harlem's many cultures. The restaurant took its name from a legendary Harlem speakeasy once located at 138th Street and 7th Avenue, where neighborhood folk, jazz greats, authors, politicians, and some of the most noteworthy figures of the twentieth century— such as Adam Clayton Powell Jr., Nat King Cole, and James

Baldwin—would converge to enjoy drinks and music in an inviting atmosphere. Since opening, Red Rooster has attracted diners from all over the world and from all walks of life—from the president of the United States to Halle Berry. Red Rooster epitomizes today's Harlem with a spirit of inclusiveness and community familiar from its distant past. His philosophy continues to inspire many audiences, across multiple platforms and even continents.

STRATEGIC TERRITORY 5: THE CULTURAL LOOP
Definition: Linking a brand with a social cause or purpose

Purpose-driven brands—those brands that put their capabilities to use in service of a pressing social problem—are often neglected by multicultural marketing. And yet research makes clear that the New Majority responds to and supports those brands that address relevant social issues—often at higher rates than the so-called general market does.

Social issues is a broad umbrella. It can encompass sustainability, health, education, equal access, civil rights, and much in between. The Cultural Loop asks the brand an unfamiliar question: What issues are most important to the community, and how can you go beyond business as usual to address them? That's much different from asking what a community wants or needs or what it ought to understand about a product or service. This approach, broadly speaking, is about responding to what matters by playing a constructive role in cultural communities. Cultural Loop strategies shift the marketing agenda from product or service promotion to community building, figuring that the karmic halo of such work will hover over the brand's balance sheet.

Caters well to: Brands with high cultural relevancy and high cultural equity.

Risk/reward: Research suggests that affinity and loyalty increase for those brands that live out a larger purpose in the world. For cultural communities in particular, the Cultural Loop can work toward building trust, demonstrating the brand's commitment to what matters and conviction to do what's best for the audience it serves. It's a vivid demonstration that the brand is not just looking to profit off the community but to build the community's good fortune.

However, good intentions are not enough. Social issues must be relevant both to the community *and* to a brand's own capabilities. Putting resources behind a certain social issue that the brand has little license to address—Cîroc Vodka, for example, has no place discussing ways to keep kids in school—makes the brand seem opportunistic and inauthentic.

American Heart Association   Blacks are nearly twice as likely to suffer from a stroke as whites are. That's a sobering statistic, made even more so when you consider this: Black death rates from stroke are higher, too. High blood pressure is also more prevalent among blacks, and although untreated high blood pressure is a major risk factor for stroke, medication and lifestyle interventions can greatly lower the risk.

The American Heart Association (AHA) has created an ongoing campaign called "Power to End Stroke" that is heavily targeted toward blacks. The aim is to reduce the incidence and severity of strokes, and although the AHA isn't a for-profit company, it has long been under fire for ignoring the needs of minorities and women. The Power to End Stroke initiative, along with "Go Red for Women" (which also has a Hispanic-oriented version), shows how a brand can use its social license to talk about an issue to create real change in multicultural communities. The result will be healthier people—and strong bonding with the brand.

Putting the Strategic Territories into Action

Once your brand has elected which strategy or strategies to pursue, it needs to build the right kind of experiences. To do that, brands need to understand the size of the opportunity, the new target audience, the customer journey, and the right channel mix. This is basic marketing blocking and tackling. The inputs may be different, but the techniques are the same for the Total Market as they are for any other marketing system. One could write a whole book on just these four points, and so I'll not derail this one by indulging in a long digression. However, I do want to remind you that you cannot rely on traditional sources of research, particularly in building the customer journeys. Moreover, keep in mind just how much more mobile first and digital first the New Majority audiences are. This may be just the moment for your brand to break its addiction to TV-first marketing.

Chapter 10

Step Five: Using Big Data to Measure Total Market Enterprise Results

If *The Graduate* were filmed today, Mr. McGuire would be telling Ben just two words: *big data*. Although "plastics," the advice Dustin Hoffman's character received in the original film, was biting commentary on the world of the time, the advice was wise. Plastics was the business of the era. Today the pot of gold is found in big data. It's used in every business, in every brand, in every marketing department, and in every technology company. Journalists mine it for interesting story angles, politicians natter on about regulation or lack thereof, privacy advocates panic about the implications of it, and, as Edward Snowden showed us, the government is quietly putting it all to use. For our purposes, big data can be used to measure the effectiveness of implementing the Total Market approach both internally and externally.

As I mentioned in Chapter 8, the practice of diversity as it is today is not enough to make an organization New Majority ready. Diversity and inclusion practices have a rather tenuous link to business performance, and it's all but impossible to measure the outcomes of these initiatives by any measure other than talent and supplier mix. As a result, these practices quantify themselves via indirect measures of talent, senior leadership training, compliance classes (constructed to keep Equal Employment

Opportunity Commission attorneys at bay), and employee retention through employee resource groups. Chief executive officers (CEOs) who apply this philosophy know they have to do it, but they have a hard time justifying the return on investment (ROI).

Just because something is difficult to measure doesn't mean it isn't worthwhile. CEOs and other senior corporate leaders are coming to realize that a diverse workforce and supplier base is good for business. They just can't prove it. Yet.

The Total Market approach uses an inside-to-outside (or inside → outside) method to measure organizations. It holds the enterprise accountable for marketplace change as a result of the change in approach. It's a cliché that you cannot improve what you cannot measure, but like most clichés, it has truth at the core. I believe that enterprise transformation is worth doing only if it can be measured. Absent that measurement, the transformation will neither blossom nor stick. Because this is so crucial to Total Market Enterprise transformation, I've developed a measurement system that peers into how an organization is moving along in not only becoming New Majority ready but also improving its marketplace position.

What Is the Total Market Enterprise Inside → Outside Strategy?

An inside → outside strategy is a corporate strategy process relying on the core competencies of the company to drive change, product development, and innovation. It is the opposite of a corporate strategy process built to adapt to external influences, such as market, competition, and customer preferences. Inside → outside adherents believe that a company achieves greater efficiencies and adapts more quickly to changing circumstances by using this technique.

It works like this: Every year, the chief talent officer (CTO) measures his or her organizational culture through an assessment or measure of his or her choice. The CEO uses this as a compass point as to whether the organization is living up to the mission, vision, and purpose of the organization. Simply put, the CTO gives the CEO a scorecard on organizational culture, which the CEO then uses to see whether the company is proceeding properly on its trajectory to serve the market as the corporate mission dictates.

A once-a-year check-in is about as effective as you imagine it to be. That's why the inside → outside strategy is predicated on ongoing compliance training, diversity workshops, and unconscious bias on the talent side while organizational design changes and budget allocations are measured on the structural end.

This kind of measurement is fairly easy to do. In fact, this data is much easier to collect and analyze than the external measures that companies invest billions in finding. There are troves of data on market performance, retailer sell through, stock keeping unit (SKU) turnover, loyalty measures, and so on.

Armed with both sets of data, a company would quickly integrate it to measure the performance of its talent against its performance in the marketplace, or so one would think. Logical, right?

So why isn't anyone doing it?

James Dix, analyst at Wedbush Securities, challenged brands at the second annual Total Market Summit. He said Wall Street is neither accurately reporting nor accurately measuring company performance. Instead, he asserted, growth is reported based on regional and geographical cycles. Many analysts are not digging into income statements to ask how companies plan to penetrate the hypergrowth segments that will account for 80 percent of U.S. population growth. They soon will, and companies that are already measuring this change will not only satisfy the analysts; they will also gain a head start in the market.

An organization measures internal performance via the following metrics:

♦ Annual talent review
♦ Performance plan
♦ 360° feedback
♦ Succession planning

Unfortunately, none of these metrics holds employees accountable for New Majority growth. The situation is much the same for external scoring as well. Enterprises measure things like the following:

♦ Market share
♦ Share price
♦ Brand metrics
♦ ROI
♦ Earnings before interest, taxes, depreciation, and amortization
♦ Compound annual growth rate

Although all of those are affected by how well the company performs in the Total Market, none of them is a direct indicator. So, how can a company measure readiness for the New Majority and correlate that to the external performance indicators that point to corporate health?

How to Implement an Inside → Outside Strategy

The answer is the Brand Cross-Cultural Matrix. The matrix combines the Brand Cross-Cultural Index (BCCI) from Chapter 8 with the Total Market Enterprise maturity model discussed in Chapters 5 and 6. An example is show in Figure 10.1.

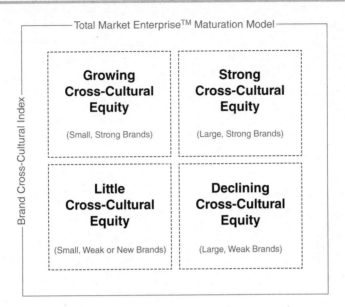

FᵢGᵤʀᴇ **10.1**   The Total Market (Inside → Outside) Matrix

This is where it all comes together—literally. The Brand Cross-Cultural Matrix combines a measure of the brand's external Total Market growth with its growing New Majority readiness.

Using this tool is simple, but I think it is a powerful at-a-glance view of how a brand stacks up in its readiness to sell to the Total Market. A brand interested in seeing where it falls would use the results of its assessment (from Chapter 6) plus its placement on the Total Market Enterprise development cycle (Chapter 7) to plot a point on the horizontal axis. Then it looks at how it ranks in the BCCI to find a level on the vertical axis. The coordinates from each of those two axes correspond to a placement within one of the four quadrants. (If your brand is not in the BCCI, use your best guess based on your own knowledge of your customer base and your sense of how your competitors interact with New Majority consumers.)

Incidentally, I've chosen to plot this against the BCCI and not the multicultural part of the index, the Multicultural Opportunity

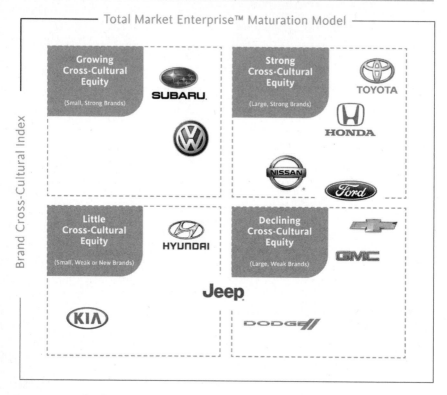

Figure 10.2 Performance of major automakers on the Cross-Cultural Matrix

(MCO). Sure, the MCO would give a brand a view about its standing with key multicultural segments, but the essence of the Total Market is to see how a brand does in relation to everyone.

To demystify this a bit more, I've plotted the major carmakers on this Cross-Cultural Matrix chart (Figure 10.2).

As you'd expect given what you've already read, Toyota is in the rarified air of the upper right corner. Honda isn't far away. However, other carmakers aren't quite as far along in either their total market development or their BCCI.

The object for any brand, automotive or not, is to move from the lower left quadrant to the upper right-hand one. Let's look at each quadrant a little more deeply.

LITTLE BRAND CROSS-CULTURAL EQUITY

Brands in the lower left quadrant score poorly on the BCCI, which means that they have limited power to influence people across all demographic segments to buy them. They may not even be particularly strong among whites. These are, invariably, small brands. They may be on their way up or their way down, and much depends on what their actions will be in the Total Market. Moreover, brands in this quadrant either are in the earliest stages of their Total Market readiness and know they have a long road ahead of them or are doing only the bare minimum necessary for compliance.

DECLINING BRAND CROSS-CULTURAL EQUITY

These are larger brands that have made headway in their development toward being Total Market ready. They do far more than comply with diversity regulations. In fact, they may already be well on their way toward Total Market maturity. However, these are brands that have not made a difference with Total Market consumers, as judged by their BCCI score. For brands in this quadrant, urgent action is needed to increase their relevance to consumers. They're already doing the right things internally, but the connection to the external market hasn't materialized.

GROWING BRAND CROSS-CULTURAL EQUITY

These are the upstarts. They're hugely relevant to Total Market consumers, but a close reading of the MCO is probably in order. They may be like Trader Joe's or Verizon—overly strong among whites and behind the times when it comes to the multicultural segments. These brands are still in the earliest (possibly the compliance) stages of their Total Market journey. Maintaining their strong, possibly leading, positions in the marketplace depends on transforming into full Total Market Enterprises. If they don't, they'll see their market positions erode as their core consumer base becomes a smaller and smaller part of the total addressable market.

STRONG BRAND CROSS-CULTURAL EQUITY

Here are the winners. It's where you want your brand to end up, and unless you're at one of the Total Market powerhouses I've already mentioned, chances are your brand isn't here yet. Brands that play here need complete Total Market maturity, and they will be seeing the impact of that in their BCCI. And that means they're also seeing it in their balance sheet. It's worth it for these brands to look closely at the ethnic segments in their MCO component score. Total Market maturation is great, but they need to make sure the connection is truly being made in a cross-cultural fashion. Are all ethnic segments feeling the love?

And if they are, well then, the sky's the limit.

Or, rather, the globe is, as you'll see in the next chapter.

Chapter **11**

What Happens in ~~2040~~ 2020 When Minorities Are the Majority?

D o you remember Y2K? There was quite a bit of freaking out, particularly among businesses. Y2K preparedness became a whole industry as enterprises hired Y2K compliance consultants to make sure their computers would survive the end of the 1900s. The clock struck midnight on January 1, 2000, and the world kept moving. I believe we're on the cusp of something similar. Brands and businesses are nervously waiting for the Y2040K phenomenon to happen. Demographers predict minorities will be the majority in the United States by 2040, and businesses are starting to realize that they need to prepare. Unlike Y2K, this change is going to have real impact, and what happens leading up to that year will determine the future of business.

What Happens in ~~2040~~ 2020?

In 2011, I executive produced a roundtable of distinguished panelists ranging from a CNN anchor to two former U.S. cabinet members, not to mention writers, activists, and business leaders. The panelists discussed where brands were in their trajectory toward tackling a New Majority world. The conclusion: Businesses are not doing enough to address the needs and services of the New Majority. Clearly, I'm not the only one ringing the alarm bells.

What are brands waiting for?

"By around 2020, more than half of the nation's children are expected to be part of a minority race or ethnic group," says National Public Radio (NPR), quoting the U.S. Census Bureau.[1] Americans under the age of 18 are at the front of a trend that will, naturally, see the overall population follow suit some 20 years later.

Another census finding states that from 2014 to 2060, "the working-age population is projected to decrease from 62 percent to 57 percent of the total population."

Here are some other Census highlights:

By 2030, 1 in 5 Americans will be age 65 or over.

The minority population is projected to rise to 56 percent of the total population in 2060, compared with 38 percent in 2014.

By 2060, the nation's foreign-born population will reach nearly 19 percent of the total population, up from 13 percent in 2014.

The "two or more races" population [mixed-race, in other words] is projected to be the fastest-growing over the next 46 years.[1]

I think you get the picture. Things are changing fast. Businesses are not adapting quickly enough. Yes, there will be a symbolic flipping of the demographic calendar in 2040, but like Y2K, businesses have to work fast starting now to prepare themselves for the change. And unlike Y2K, this is not a sudden event. The demographic changes are already profound and are growing more so every day. The time to adapt is not 2040. It is today.

Let's start by discussing the generations marketers are concerned with.

The Three Generations

There are three major age cohorts that compose the U.S. adult population. Although the boundaries that separate them are not exact, these crude groupings allow us to draw some broad conclusions about the characteristics of each age tranche, as you can see in Table 11.1.

I mentioned earlier in the case study about life insurance that in New Majority households, we often found three generations living together. Incidentally, we also found that the New Majority also includes the underserved and underbanked communities. Nearly a decade after the Great Recession, we find that the makeup of family has a different meaning when you include socioeconomic data and the growth of gender-neutral households.

TABLE 11.1 Characteristics of major demographic cohorts

Characteristic	Millennials	Generation X	Baby Boomers
Age	21–35	30–50	51–69
2015 Pop. Share	24.6%	15.3%	23.3%
Median Household Income	$52,000 (Age 25–34)	$64,000 (Age 35–44)	$62,000 (Age 45–64)
Education	63.7% completed some college	61.7% completed some college	58% completed some college
Attitude	Trend setting, experience driven, work–life balance, optimistic	Pessimistic, skeptical, moderate	Quality driven, pessimistic about future
Behavior	Tech savvy, personal goal-oriented, more progressive	Self-reliant, savvy	Juggling career, family, and personal life; risk averse

In the end, we produced for our insurance client a campaign about the Conversation. You know, the one conversation no one likes to have. The talk about death. Multigenerational New Majority households have the conversation about death in their own unique ways, and our life insurer was able to augment that. They were able to respond to the New Majority marketplace demands with a new product built specifically based on new insights.

Life insurance isn't the only thing that will change. These demographic shifts are already producing major changes in the composition of consumer products and services. Many of the service models that exist today will be in a fight for survival. The millennial generation will be the one deciding the outcome. Not only is it the most diverse generation in America, but it is also about to take over from the baby boomer generation as the largest, as shown in Figure 11.1.

The impact on product development is mind-blowing. Take, for example, the Internet of Things. It is changing the way homes are being built for new millennial home owners.

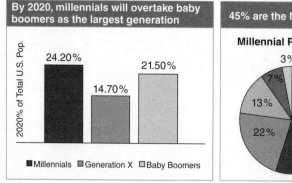 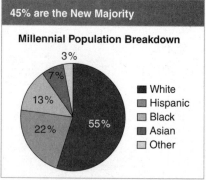

FIGURE 11.1   Millennial—The Biggest and Most Diverse Generation

Source: Mintel, *Marketing to Millennials—US—February 2014*, February 2014; Experian Marketing Services, *Millennials Come of Age*, June 2014.

While I was in the strategy group at Whirlpool, we tried to make the refrigerator the center of the connected home. It failed because the industry was trying to market to Generation Xers— my generation. Gen X was the first generation to experience readily available desktop and laptop computers. Not everyone within the Generation X cycle took advantage of technology, of course. But damn near every single millennial consumer grew up with that kind of technology . . . and more.

Speaking of growing up, many brands and businesses think millennials are just graduating or staying at home with Mom and Dad. In fact, there are two main groupings in the generation. They're so distinct that I question why we even consider them the same generation. The older millennials are age 30 to 38 whereas their younger counterparts are anywhere between ages 21 and 29. But both parts of the generation are remarkable. Millennials are the most educated and, because the economy finally recovered, most employed generation around (see Figure 11.2). They will soon become the dominant age cohort in the workplace.

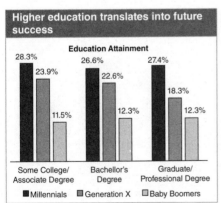

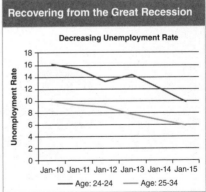

FIGURE 11.2 Most Educated and Working More

Source: Mintel, *Marketing to Millennials—US—February 2014*, Mintel February 2014; Bureau of Labor Statistics.

Millennials are beginning to reach the different milestones in life.

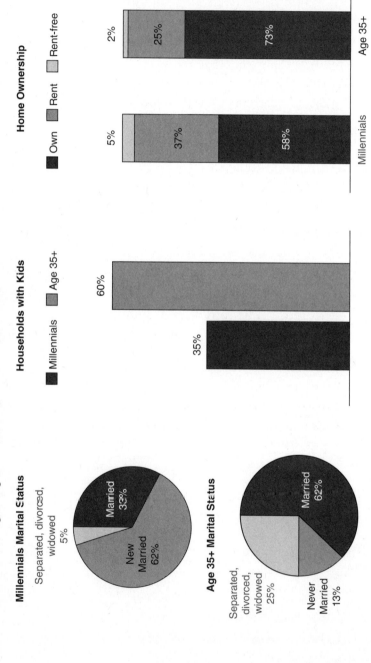

FIGURE 11.3 Life rolling along slowly

Life is rolling along slowly for these folks. They are coming of age. Older millennials are predominantly unmarried and have kids in the home, while those ages 21 to 34 are married more often than not but have kids at only about half the rate of their older peers. And lest you think they don't have kids because they're still in the basement rec room at home, let these numbers change your mind. Only 5 percent of millennials are still at home. A third of them are renters, and nearly 60 percent own their own homes.

Why tell you all of this? Because products and services are about to undergo a revolution to meet the needs of this new, giant generation. The changes that the baby boomers wrought on the United States are due for a sequel.

New Majority millennials are a subsegment—an enormous subsegment—of the millennial generation. Their likes and dislikes drive decisions in product categories such as automobiles, food, beverage, travel, hotels, and housing.

That last one is especially interesting. Home improvement is undergoing serious changes right now.

In 2009, right after the Great Recession, Home Depot was exploring ways to grow. The economic downturn meant that growth could not come from opening new stores. The brand got smart and looked in a new place for growth: black women who were heads of households. Why? Black women have the highest growth rate of college-educated heads of households in the United States. Lowe's saw part of the same trend and launched a general-market, female-focused strategy in the early 2000s, which changed its overall store format and placement of product on shelves.

Home Depot took it a step further. They looked beyond suburban, white households and dug deeper at the local geographic and demographic level.

Home Depot partnered with the comedian Steve Harvey and his multiplatform media company to offer helpful do-it-yourself tips for home repair directly targeted at black female heads of households. The brand combined data and insights to create an experience specific to the New Majority subsegment, and it did it with geotargeted communications across digital platforms. Very sophisticated stuff.

The changes don't stop there. Personal health, travel, time management, giving back to the community, living close to friends and family, having new experiences, and giving their children a better future—these are all important areas millennial consumers care more about than other generations do (see Figure 11.4).

Airbnb is a disruptor of the leisure-travel category based on millennial wants and needs. Airbnb is a successful model because it understood the millennial desire for technology, sharing, and

MILLENNIALS CARE MORE ABOUT

- Personal health
- Travel
- Time management
- Giving back to the community
- Living close to with friends and family
- Having new experiences
- Giving their children a better future

Figure 11.4 Life-First Mentality

Source: Mintel, *Marketing to Millennials—US—February 2014*, Mintel February 2014; Council of Economic Advisors, *15 Economic Facts about Millennials*, October 2014.

personalization. Unlike Generation X and the baby boomer generation, millennials have a life-first mentality.

But the surge in travel is unequally distributed across the millennial generation. The growth in U.S. Hispanic, black, and Asian travelers is far outpacing the white, non-Hispanic consumer. Approximately 31 percent of Hispanics travel in a group of four or more, compared with 25 percent in the population as a whole. Hispanics are more likely to travel with children and to travel with more than two adults than the general population.[2]

This was a great thing for Airbnb. The company was first to market with the use of technology and personalization in hospitality. Its radical new model addresses the millennial idea of life balance, making travel sharable and personal. It is a global insight to offer accommodations to travelers to stay with families and individuals while creating an additional revenue stream through the shared experience.

Take for instance, Harlem, New York. It is Airbnb's third-largest market. Why? Harlem has long been known as a cultural mecca and well-known brand the world over. It also suffers from being an underserved market when it comes to hotels. Because Harlem is a global brand, it attracts travelers from Paris, Italy, and Germany, to name a few. On Sundays you cannot find a clear path on the sidewalk or score a restaurant reservation at Sylvia's.

Buses arrive at churches full of European travelers looking to get a taste of the new Harlem Renaissance. It is a region of New York that has the Hispanic experience in East Harlem, the black and culinary experience in Central Harlem, and a world-class education and medical experience in West Harlem. It also has very few hotels. Who fills the void within a New Majority region within New York? Airbnb.

The formula is fairly simple. Understand the total addressable market opportunity while including the New Majority. Make sure your talent not only reflects the audience you service but is also incentivized to be brave and go deep with understanding the New Majority. Only then can you create experiences relevant to them, make the business case to shift internal resources and assets to match the population, and put systems in place that are not driven by white attitudes. You can choose to test your cultural assumptions or just go all-in like Beats, Airbnb, Uber, and other New Majority–friendly products did.

Parents Just Don't Understand

Millennials aren't the only generation worth discussing, of course. Although Generation X may draw the short straw, the millennials—especially New Majority millennials—are becoming parents in huge numbers.

If the world of the millennials is crazily different, imagine the type of kids they are having. Some call them Generation Z, but there is no broadly agreed-upon name for this cohort. Similar to their Generation X and millennial parents, Generation Z is a minority majority generation. In fact, they are the real standard-bearers. Generation Z is the first generation to be more than 50 percent minority.

Gen Zers seem to prefer in-person to online interaction and are being schooled in emotional intelligence from a young age. Thanks to social media, they are accustomed to engaging with friends all over the world. They will be well prepared for a global business environment, if they can ever get their heads out of Minecraft.

What Will Generation Z Mean to Brands and Businesses?

Gen Z's parents are familiar with the Internet, and most, but not all, have an understanding of social media. Gen Zers themselves have a native understanding of social media and take the Internet for granted.

I think that Gen Z really is the first digital-native generation. Many children and young teens have been using apps on smartphones and tablets since they were old enough to hold the devices. Likewise, social media networks have always been part of their world.

Brands with products or services for this audience are in a huge dilemma. Their core consumers are usually white and non-Hispanic. The brands have to protect their base with insights and research methodologies, all of which will fade into irrelevance in as little as a decade.

Brands that market to middle-school-age kids or even kids zero to five years old have to change the mind-set of their entire enterprises. In 2014 Kimberly-Clark launched an initiative aimed at the growing multicultural-mom population. This was one of the industry's first Total Market executions.

I was confused that the industry was confused by the notion that a major brand would lead with New Majority insights within a category that's already New Majority. Fifty-one percent of kids zero to two are already New Majority. What's the big deal?

Look at headlines from a major industry publication:

Kimberly-Clark's New Hispanic Program Aims at General Market

Celebrate Family Unity Includes Customized Family Song App, Singer Christina Milian

> —*Advertising Age*, April 2014

A campaign like that won't even rate a small story by 2020. The New Majority is here today, right now, especially for kids and teens. Follow the Total Market approach, and your brand and business will win in the marketplace.

Chapter 12

Implementing the Total Market Approach around the World

B ack in 2009 a group of us were researching the meaning of cross-culturalism in preparation for the work we were soon to do with brands. We ran across a different word—one that seemed more like the inchoate thing we were looking to express: *transcultural*. Transculturalism, we learned, is rooted in the pursuit of shared interests and common values across cultural and national borders. That word, especially for the global agency in which we worked, seemed perfect. And yet we discarded it, choosing instead to go with a weaker, yet more apt word: *cross-cultural*. Cross-culturalism is concerned with *exchange beyond the boundaries* of the nation or cultural group. In short, it is a celebration of values and beliefs across cultural groups. We chose to go with *cross-cultural* because we thought it was the best description of where the United States was at that moment in its history.

I still believe that the current cross-cultural time is a developmental phase on our national journey toward transculturalism. I believe that because it's happened before.

As all of us learned in school, the United States experienced a great wave of immigration in the latter half of the nineteenth century and the early part of the twentieth. During that time, the foreign-born population of the United States hovered around

13 to 14 percent of the total (reaching a peak of 14.7 percent in 1910, nearly two percentage points higher than today), with the vast majority (85 to 90 percent, depending on the year) of those people coming from different regions in Europe. And they were young, with the median age of the foreign born around 35 years—just about what it is today. Some 25 million Europeans came to the United States, and even though they were predominantly white, they were as culturally distinct as any of the New Majority populations are today—perhaps even more so.

Advertising and marketing was not then what it is today (and neither were corporations), but had it been, the old-guard U.S. population would have been seen as the general market while those German, Slavic, Irish, and Jewish newcomers would have been seen as the multicultural element. These populations both kept to themselves and mixed with other immigrants. Their kids did less of the former and more of the latter. They were forged together as a nation by war, and with the unheralded contributions of America's blacks, they gave birth to modern American culture. In the process, these distinct societies began as individual cultures, passed through a cross-cultural stage, and eventually emerged as a transcultural nation.

The latest wave of immigration (both from foreign countries and via internal movement) has given America a new opportunity to refresh its culture. We're cross-cultural now, but we'll become a different sort of transcultural nation soon.

International Transculturalism

I've spent the last six years developing the Total Market model from a communications perspective into an enterprise transformation tool. But part of working at the enterprise level is grappling with the needs of global corporations.

Unsurprisingly, I've long been asked whether the Total Market approach could be applied globally. I chuckled when I was asked because I think the concept we settled on—cross-cultural—is more applicable globally than it is in the soon-to-be transcultural United States.

Because of the rising middle class, global female emancipation and empowerment, burgeoning youth populations, and increasing religious devotion, brands and businesses face massive uncertainty about their place in the global future.

One of those uncertain companies was Kodak, and it was the first client to sign up for the Cross-Cultural Practice. It was 2009, and Kodak was a brand in search of relevancy. (Today, after bankruptcy, it is a brand in search of value in its vast trove of patents and technologies.)

Kodak was in a fight for its life because of changing technology and demographics. A bit of research revealed that Hispanic and black consumers (ages 18–24) were the most frequent users of the cameras on their cell phones. That rate was only going to increase, and it was going to be a global problem. So we were asked to assess a campaign designed to drive Kodak sales and positive brand attributes in the United States, India, Europe, and South America. We judged it cross-culturally effective, and Kodak pushed it out from North America to the rest of the world. But it was still too late for Kodak.

The approach we took with Kodak in 2009 was typical for a brand looking to deliver a global campaign. Start in the West—often the United States—and localize the campaign for other countries. It usually works like this: A global brand asks an agency to help it build a global positioning, which the agency develops based on qualitative or quantitative research either from people on the ground or through a third-party database.

The research is run through the general-market lens or the majority population within individual countries. The agency then comes back and presents a strategic platform for the brand. That strategic platform is localized so that the brand can have the same or similar meaning across the world. This means the brand shows up consistently throughout the world, which is exactly what global brand managers are after. This West-to-East model worked when the bulk of global wealth was in the United States and when nearly every country in the world aspired to the Western lifestyle.

That's changing. Let's start with China. The world's second-largest economy won't be in that slot for long. It's growing enormously, and a massive middle class is developing there. They're urbanizing and starting to flex their consumer muscle. Growth is returning to India, while Brazil is finally looking to deliver on its promise of being the country of the future. And there are many other countries—Mexico, Indonesia, Nigeria, Vietnam, and others—where a large and robust middle class is emerging. Great swathes of the global population are emerging into something more than substance living, and a new global consumer class is being born. Race and ethnicity do create internal cultural pockets within all the fast-growing countries, but what drives global cross-culturalism is the middle class, women, youth, and religion.

Remember the British Airways film I mentioned earlier in the book? To create it, Ogilvy & Mather had to dig into regional and local nuances. We had to interpret the strategy and the brand meaning to the Asian Indian consumer looking to fly back to India. We did not and could not apply the Western approach to the Eastern consumer mind-set.

What changed while using the Total Market approach and cross-cultural insights? Nothing. We used the same steps: Assess the organization's understanding of its New Majority, cross-cultural insight development, customer journeys and personas, contact strategy, and the brief and effectiveness plan.

When we began to dig into the existing global campaign, we noticed we had to look deeply into the local market to understand subsegments, such as religious preferences, class, career progression, and marital status. We found and used nuances that were specific to regional and local markets and highlighted signal experiences that we learned U.S. South Asian middle-class and upper-middle-class consumers craved. And we did it all through technology. We deployed video and social customer care across both global markets and watched as the results exceeded expectations and drove category growth.

Not every global brand is ready to deploy the Total Market and cross-cultural approach. In the case of one global hair care brand, my practice was selected over a few good multicultural agencies. My closing line for the pitch was "If you were looking for a multicultural agency, then you should hire a multicultural agency." We were offering something different.

What happened after the pitch was life changing—at least for me. I saw the power of using a new approach to a very tried yet profitable category: ethnic hair products. When you think of ethnic hair products in the United States, you think of Madam C. J. Walker, the inventor of ethnic hair products distributed en masse. It's a multibillion-dollar industry.

This global brand wanted us to build its market in both the United States and Africa. In Africa, we were marketing to a growing middle class. In the United States, black hair care and styling were shifting from using chemical-based products (perms) and began to prefer a more natural look.

The shift was having a significant impact on a newly acquired brand in the larger company's hair portfolio. After using the cross-cultural approach both in the United States and globally, we knew we could not come back to the enterprise with a typical West-to-East global platform. Instead we recommended a texture-based approach. Instead of selling hair products based on ethnicity, we'd sell the whole portfolio based on texture—kinky, curly, wavy, or straight.

To our surprise, we were met with resistance. Shifting the new ethnic brand to a texture-based offering meant reshuffling all of the hair care brands. The global company just didn't believe that a newly acquired brand could now cast a wider customer base by shifting from ethnic-based to texture-based products, and it certainly didn't believe it was worth the complicated shift of its whole existing portfolio. Imagine the implications. No more ethnic aisles of products that get little to no attention or shelf presence. What the global brand failed to understand was that the approach we recommended didn't mean the dismantling of ethnic products and an incipient threat to some of its biggest sellers. Instead, we were proposing to expand a relevant suite of products, armed with the right product development budget, appropriate prices, and distribution in all the right places for the New Majority. But the company was not ready for the Total Market approach using cross-cultural communications.

Where Do We Go from Here?

The Total Market approach is not going anywhere. It's like asking whether the United States will go back to having segregated schools. The current general-market and multicultural models have been the only options for the past 50 years. That made sense for decades, but it doesn't anymore. I've spent the last six years proving the rightness of the Total Market approach and working to demonstrate how this goes beyond marketing and communications. My goal, really, is to change the way business is done.

It's going to have to change. I mentioned Kodak at the beginning of this chapter. As you know, shortly after my involvement with it ended, the company went bankrupt. (Not my fault!) Looking back, I can see parallels between what did happen to

Kodak and what may happen to companies that ignore the Total Market. Kodak invented digital photography—the very thing that killed it in a neat example of technological patricide. Kodak, as has been written about a gazillion times, did not understand the existential threat that digital photography posed. Kodak was in the memory business. It gave people the means to make and keep memories. Digital cameras—especially smartphones—meant that consumers could make the same kind of tangible memories without using (or paying) Kodak.

The problem wasn't that Kodak didn't understand this. It would have had to be a fool to miss the implications of digital photography, and it was anything but a fool. But it failed to wean itself off the massive profits of the film business in time. By the time that business was declining, the digital-photography business had passed Kodak by. It saw the coming change, but the company couldn't grapple with the short-term revenue implications and organizational redesign necessary to meet it. The short-term profits were just too high to get Kodak to change in time.

Many businesses, I believe, are at a similar inflection point now. The profits from the general market are still great. The disruption necessary to become a Total Market Enterprise is great as well. But those companies that invest in the shift will win in the Total Market era. I'm excited about what's to come.

If at any time you need help with your brand or business, reach out to me at www.reframethebrand.com. And if you need a quick refresher on the book, just find your way back here to this quick summary of what's inside.

Book Summary

In Chapter 1, I explained why the Total Market approach to marketing can make you a more efficient and more effective marketer, manager, or corporate executive. I shared the origins of the Total Market approach with traditional methodologies and provided an overview of the steps involved in the Total Market marketing process.

In Chapter 2, I shared how changing demographic patterns are reshaping America. We're on our way to becoming a country of majority minorities (in essence, the New Majority, in which whites will be the largest plurality). Americans now come in more shades of human than ever before. The growth of these formerly overlooked segments coincides with the development of powerful research tools, enabling us to identify and weight different buying triggers among and within groups with more precision than was previously possible. The convergence of these factors is what makes the Total Market approach both valid and necessary.

In Chapter 3, I shared my view about how brands and businesses must tear down the general market and multicultural wall. Today and since the inception of the industry, there's been a general-market and a multicultural approach to the market. Both approaches are dated. If the United States can amend its relations with Cuba, the marketing and communications industry can evolve. We explored how the approaches formed, discussed pros and cons to both approaches, and made the case for why both approaches do not drive maximum value for brands and businesses.

Chapter 4 provided examples of Total Market efforts. Advertising creative is not the only outcome of the Total

Market approach. In part, it's a statement for changing the perspective, of seeing things and doing things differently.

Chapter 5 was a demonstration of the tools you can use to take a Total Market approach using your current staff and vendors. It discussed how you can bring Total Market thinking to your office, your department, or your division.

The second half of the book was all about breaking down the five key steps for becoming a Total Market Enterprise.

In Chapter 6, I shared how to assess the organization before diving into a Total Market approach. Not every organization is New Majority ready. I gave key nuggets for understanding where your organization is right now.

In Chapter 7, I gave you my reasons for why the current diversity and inclusion model will not work within the New Marketplace. I shared best practices and tools for getting your organizational structure ready.

Chapter 8 is the most important chapter in the book. Here you found a new tool you could use to determine where your company's weaknesses were in the Total Market landscape. It showed you an approach to figure out how much money brands are leaving on the table by not appealing to the Total Market.

Chapters 9 and 10 go hand in hand. It's hard to design the new customer experience for the New Majority without understanding your measurement and performance plan. Customer engagement is the new *it* marketing concept, and new tools mean you can reach national and local consumers with similar exactitude and accountability.

In the last few chapters of the book, I shared a perspective about what happens to brands and businesses in 2020.

(*continued*)

(*continued*)

Brands cannot wait until 2040 to change. The world is not going to end, but without the right preparation, you will lose market share to a competitor that's better prepared for the New Majority.

Finally, we come to this chapter, my good-bye, for now at least. If you need help with your Total Market transformation or just have questions, check out my website, www.reframethebrand.com, or reach out to me via e-mail (jeffrey.bowman@reframethebrand.com) or Twitter (@jeffreyl bowman). I'd love to hear from you.

Cheers.

Notes

Chapter 1

1. Powell, Brian, Catherine Bolzendahl, Claudia Geist, and Lala Carr Steelman. *Counted Out: Same-Sex Relations and Americans Definitions of Family*. New York: Russell Sage Foundation, 2010.

2. Duggan, Bill. "What Is Total Market? AHAA Helps Provide a Definition!" *Marketing Maestros* (blog). May 2, 2014. http://www.ana.net/blogs/show/id/30414.

Chapter 2

1. Porter, Michael E. "The Competitive Advantage of the Inner City." *Harvard Business Review*, May/June 1995, 55–71.

Chapter 3

1. David Ogilvy. *Ogilvy on Advertising*. New York: Vintage Books, 1985, 26.

2. Association of National Advertisers. "About the ANA." Accessed June 15, 2015. http://www.ana.net/about.

3. Ibid.

Chapter 4

1. Seddon, Joanna. "The Brand in the Boardroom: Making the Case for Investment in Brand." Edited by Carla Hendra and Jeremy Katz. *Red Papers* 6 (November 2013).

2. Wyndham Worldwide. "Mission & Culture." Accessed June 15, 2015. http://www.wyndhamworldwide.com/category/mission-culture.

Chapter 9

1. Jones, Tao. "Upfronts 2015: Black—and Hispanic and Asian—Are the New Black on Primetime Network TV." *Speakeasy* (blog). *Wall Street Journal.* May 13, 2015. http://blogs.wsj.com/speakeasy/2015/05/13/upfronts-2015-black-and-hispanic-and-asian-are-the-new-black-on-primetime-network-tv/.

Chapter 11

1. Colby, Sandra L., and Jennifer M. Ortman. *Projections of the Size and Composition of the U.S. Population: 2014 to 2060.* Current Population Reports (P25–1143). Washington, DC: U.S. Census Bureau, 2014. Quoted in Bill Chappell. "For U.S. Children, Minorities Will Be the Majority by 2020, Census Says." NPR. March 4, 2015. http://www.npr.org/sections/thetwo-way/2015/03/04/390672196/for-u-s-children-minorities-will-be-the-majority-by-2020-census-says.

2. Mandala Research. Quoted in National Tour Association. *Hispanic Travel Market: Reference Guide.* Lexington, KY: NTA. Accessed June 16, 2015. www.ntaonline.com/includes/media/docs/Hispanic-2014.pdf.

About the Author

**Jeffrey L. Bowman, Author,
Founder and Chairman of
REFRAME: The Brand**
www.jeffreylbowman.com |
@jeffreylbowman |
www.reframethebrand.com |
@reframethebrand

Jeffrey L. Bowman is an author, as well as the Founder and
Chairman of REFRAME: The Brand, a platform conceived to
prepare executives for the New Majority. The organization provides Total Market Enterprise™ advisory, education, and training
through a software as a service (SaaS) platform. Since launching
the organization in 2013, Bowman has grown it from 61 members
to more than 200 members.

As a former Senior Partner and Managing Director at Ogilvy &
Mather, one of the world's largest advertising and communications agencies, Bowman pioneered a new communications
model that not only bridged the general market and multicultural
marketing communications approaches, but also redefined
change management. Today, he leads the industry charge in
transforming brands and businesses for the New Majority.

Author of the highly acclaimed *Cross-Cultural Report* and
Brand Cross-Cultural Index, two firsts for the industry, Bowman
is advertising's most recognized pioneering thought leader and
practitioner on the Total Market approach. This new industry
category challenges the antiquated approach to marketing and

advertising developed in the 1950s and taps into all the new and emerging consumer segments that are currently transforming the world's population.

A true strategist and visionary, Bowman is known for change management and marketing effectiveness work with global brands such as British Petroleum, British Airways, Coca-Cola, Campbell's, Gap, IKEA, Kimberly-Clark, SC Johnson, Mass Mutual, MetLife, PepsiCo, Unilever, United Airlines, Verizon, and Wyndham, among others. His pioneering work in reframing the marketplace has been covered in the *New York Times*, *Advertising Age*, and *The Economist*.

Bowman lives in New York City with his wife and two daughters.

Index

Note: Page references in *italics* refer to figures.